PARADISE LOST

THE UNIVERSITY OF QUEENSLAND PRESS
SCHOLARS' LIBRARY

PARADISE LOST
A Humanist Approach

K.G. Hamilton

University of
Queensland Press
St Lucia·London·New York

© University of Queensland Press, St Lucia, Queensland 1981
Second Printing, 1983

This book is copyright. Apart from any fair dealing for the
purposes of private study, research, criticism, or review, as
permitted under the Copyright Act, no part may be reproduced
by any process without written permission. Enquiries should be
made to the publishers.

Typeset by University of Queensland Press
Printed and bound by The Dominion Press—Hedges & Bell, Melbourne

Distributed in the United Kingdom, Europe, the Middle East,
Africa, and the Caribbean by Prentice-Hall International,
International Book Distributors Ltd., 66 Wood Lane End,
Hemel Hempstead, Herts., England

*National Library of Australia
Cataloguing-in-Publication data*

Hamilton, K.G. (Kenneth Gordon), 1921–
    Paradise lost.

    Bibliography.
    Includes index.
    ISBN 0 7022 1626 7.

    1. Milton, John, 1608–1674. Paradise lost –
Criticism and interpretation. I. Title.

821'.4

"What really interests me is whether in creating the world God had any choice."

Albert Einstein

"I paint these religious subjects because in them I find a great deal of humanity."

Pietro Annigoni

Contents

Publisher's Note

As the costs of labor-intensive book production have risen astronomically over the past few years, it has become increasingly difficult to produce short print run scholarly books at a reasonable price. This book is in a series designed by the University of Queensland Press to make available such reference and specialist works.

Books in the series will be set on an IBM Electronic Composer and of necessity certain refinements, such as superscript footnote numbers and costly jackets, will be replaced by cheaper substitutes. Ordinarily they will not be stocked by booksellers and may be obtained by writing directly to the publisher.

The University of Queensland Press hopes that its Scholars' Library will be recognized by the scholarly and specialist community as a genuine effort to preserve the important role of the specialist book.

Preface

It has been said of Shakespeare's *Hamlet* that it needs to be reinterpreted for each successive generation of readers. This may be going rather too far; but as regards *Paradise Lost* it could be time for a wider look at its meaning for the present-day reader. The last really influential large scale reinterpretation was perhaps A. J. A. Waldock's *Paradise Lost and Its Critics* (1947), which was to some extent a rebuttal of the poem's traditional reading by C. S. Lewis in his *Preface to Paradise Lost* (1942). Since then there have been such radical readings as William Empson's *Milton's God* (1961), a number of attempts to explain, or explain away, the difficulties that arise for twentieth-century readers attempting to approach the poem in an orthodox way, notably Isabel McCaffrey's *Paradise Lost as Myth* (1959) and S. E. Fish's *Surprised by Sin* (1967), as well as virtually innumerable treatments of more or less limited aspects of the poem, its background, critical history, and so on.

This present book does not set out to rewrite the *Paradise Lost* literature. It is one essentially for students of Milton, though I would hope that Milton scholars, if I may make the distinction, will also find things to interest them in it, as well as things to disagree with. It has been written out of a good many years of experience of teaching Milton to English Honours students, but I am hopeful that readers of *Paradise Lost* at all levels, including those who are still lucky enough to come across the poem at school and those who read it simply for pleasure may find the book readable and helpful. I have concentrated as far as possible on the poem itself, with little direct reference to secondary reading, either as source material or criticism, leaving the reader to pursue these matters for himself, perhaps using the Bibliography as a starting point. What I have tried to do is to analyze, on the evidence of the poem's own words, what I see as its meaning for the present-day reader. I might also say that though I have written primarily for those who are already familiar with the poem, it would be my hope to lead some who have only a slighter acquaintance with it to know it better. I have therefore endeavoured to write in a way that will be at least intelligible to the latter; though at the same time expecting that the more intimate the knowlege of the poem the more interesting and rewarding the essays are likely to be.

The book, then, is intended to present a personal view of *Paradise Lost*.

I would make this point now, once and for all, in order that I should not have to make similar qualifications throughout the course of the work. By claiming it as a personal view I do not mean to say that everything in it is original. Far from it. Much of what I have to say is more or less traditional. But I would none the less hope that the book as a whole represents a fresh approach to the poem; although I would again hasten to add that I do not see this approach as in any way exclusive, or as precluding other different approaches. *Paradise Lost* is large enough to accommodate more than one view. Indeed I would claim that a major fault in much Milton criticism has arisen from critics misleading themselves into thinking that the whole imaginative structure of the poem, or large parts of it, can be interpreted completely from a single point of view, with the inevitable result that the point of view becomes the master and the poem is distorted to fit into it. Being aware of the danger does not insure that one will escape it; but my hope is that in what I have written I have confined myself to an honest attempt to understand the poem and to help towards a greater pleasure and satisfaction to be gained from its reading.

The same danger of distorting the poem in the interests of developing an extended thesis regarding it was perhaps the main cause leading to a preference for a series of essays rather than a monograph. The essay series, particularly if it is understood in its original meaning of "attempts on" a subject, is especially suited to the discussion of a complex major work such as *Paradise Lost*. It allows the poem to be seen from a variety of points of view, and the discussion in each case need be pursued no further than it can profitably be taken from that point of view, each essay providing the opportunity for a fresh start. At the same time I would hope for a certain degree of unity coming from the concentration of all the essays on the poem itself; and also from an overall attitude to the poem which sees it being best understood by the twentieth-century reader as a work with a strong humanistic element — an attitude which, while serving to hold the essays together in a relatively loose way, does not I would hope unduly impose itself on them.

There has, however, been one major difficulty emerging from this choice of the essay form. Because the poem is itself a unity, aspects of it cannot readily be separated out and treated in isolation. A certain amount of repetition between essays has, therefore, been inevitable, though I have tried to meet this as far as possible by treating each matter most fully in the context which seemed most convenient, and referring to it only briefly in other contexts where it might arise. In this way I hope I have avoided undue repetition, while at the same time maintaining as far as possible the autonomy of individual essays. Another consequence of the essay form, which however I am not particularly worried about, is inconsistency. When a work as complex as *Paradise Lost* is looked at from different points of view a certain amount of inconsistency is likely; indeed if it did not appear one might suspect that the poem was being lost sight of in the interests of consistency. To use an image from the poet Archibald Macleish, the true meaning of the poem is not in any single interpretation, any single image, but "in the space between".

I mentioned earlier that the book had its origins in the teaching of *Paradise Lost* to Honours students, and in writing it I have necessarily to acknowledge a considerable debt to my students over the years, ranging from ideas I have developed under the pressure of seminar discussion, to material that I have been able to incorporate into the essays more or less directly from the students' own work. In most cases I cannot isolate the contribution made by individual students. I would however make particular mention of Bruce Nash, for some of the key ideas in the essay on the war in Heaven, and of Ann Collett, for her contribution to the material for the essay on the fall. Also Elizabeth Dickson and Penny Smith — indeed there are many others I could mention, but my main debt to the students is a more general one. Without the impetus of their interest in *Paradise Lost* over the years this book certainly would not have been written.

I also indicated that there is much in the essays that is not original, in the sense that it, or something like it, has been said before. But to attempt to acknowledge individually every debt in a work like this would not only be extremely cumbersome, it would also be impossible. Over a period, ideas gained from reading become part of the texture of one's own thinking and the barrier between what is original to oneself and what is not becomes very blurred. I would therefore acknowledge a general debt to Milton scholars whose work has helped in the formation of my understanding of the poem, including all those listed in the Bibliography. I would mention here, however, Margaret Mahood's *Poetry and Humanism* and Arnold Stein's *Answerable Style* for the formative influence they had on my approach to *Paradise Lost*. I owe a debt, too, which must be acknowledged to Dr Beverley Sherry, who assisted with the Bibliography as well as cooperating with me in the teaching of Milton over a number of years; and also to Cecil Hadgraft and Robert McQuitty, who read much of the manuscript and made many valuable suggestions.

Because I am not here concerned with textual problems I have thought it most convenient to quote throughout from a text using modern spelling. The actual text used is *The Poems of John Milton* edited by Carey and Fowler (Longmans, 1968).

St Lucia   **K. G. H.**
1980

1

Introduction

There is no single work of English Literature, even including, say, *Hamlet* or *King Lear,* which so consistently or so surely rouses the interest of readers as does *Paradise Lost*; and this despite a general antipathy towards the poem before it is actually read. My main purpose in these essays is to explore why this should be so, to uncover the special significance and interest of *Paradise Lost* for the present-day reader. That is to say, I am perhaps more concerned to do this than I am, by concentrating on the origins of the poem in seventeenth-century attitudes, beliefs and traditions, to help the reader to understand it specifically in its seventeenth-century context, to assist him to become one of the "fit audience though few" for whom Milton was conscious of himself as writing.

But this needs some qualification. At the risk of becoming involved in that critical bugbear, the intentional fallacy, my belief is that a reader can claim to be understanding, to be responding adequately to a poem only if his response has some reference to his own experience *and* if that reference has some overlap with an experience, conscious or unconscious, which the poet could reasonably be seen as striving to express. The reader does not, I would say, have an entirely free hand to interpret a poem in whatever way it strikes him. Or to put it in another way, if the exercise of that freedom results in an interpretation manifestly contrary to anything the poet could be expected to have intended, this will cast doubt on the adequacy of the interpretation, and suggest the need for a more searching look at it. William Empson's vastly entertaining *Milton's God* is often invalid or unsatisfying for this reason. It is not necessarily that the words of the poem cannot be read in the way he suggests, although very often, I think, this is only possible at best by completely ignoring the rest of the poem and taking individual lines and passages in isolation. Rather it is simply impossible to accept Milton's having written the poem as Empson wants us to read it, unless indeed he were inspired not as he claimed by the Holy Spirit but by Satan himself!

The essays that follow, then, are based broadly on the assumption that *Paradise Lost* is not, as it has been called, a monument to dead ideas but, like all great works of literature, a living thing, an organism with a life of its own, not altogether independent of its origin but owing much to the environment in which it has lived and is living. And it is with the poem as it lives today that I am primarily concerned. If I might provide a minor example by way of illustration, the word *pandemonium* was coined by Milton as a name for the meeting place of the fallen angels after their arrival in Hell, the place "of all the devils", on the same model (without any intentional witticism) as such modern coinages as "Pan American". It seems to have had no wider meaning than this for Milton, and the *OED* does not find examples of its use with some of its present-day connotations until more than a century later. But I am sure that few readers would want to exclude these connotations from their reading of the particular passage simply because Milton could not have intended them. The fact is that the wider meaning has developed in the process of growth of the language, and in doing so has become part of the growth of the poem, enriching the passage without in any way dislocating or detracting from its original meaning. However it should be realized that it can do this only because the present-day meaning of the word is in a direct line of descent or development from the meaning with which Milton used it, because the potential for this meaning was indeed always there. This means that it is necessary to know what the word originally meant for Milton in order to be sure that a modern reading of it is within its potentiality for development; and my objection to many of Empson's ideas about the poem is that it is impossible, for me at least, either to impute them to Milton or to see them as having developed from anything that could be imputed to him.

What applies in this minor example of the word *pandemonium* may apply also to other more fundamental aspects of the poem, including the beliefs, attitudes, moral systems and so on, which it includes. These things change and develop in time as does language, and it is one of the tests of a great work of literature that it should be able to grow and develop with them. A *Paradise Lost* tied closely to the tenets of seventeenth-century puritan ideas and beliefs might be historically interesting, but it would not have the continuing breadth of appeal of Milton's poem. It is simply because the poem can be read in terms of twentieth-century preoccupations, without being untrue to its seventeenth-century origins, that it retains its position as the major work of earlier English literature most likely to inspire lasting interest among present-day readers.

An important clue towards an understanding of why *Paradise Lost* should continue to interest readers who no longer accept many of the attitudes and beliefs on which it is ostensibly based is to be found in an understanding of the term *Christian humanism*. The label *Christian humanist* has been widely applied to Milton without, I think, sufficient consideration of the paradoxical implications inherent in the concept of Christian humanism itself, implications made clear by the respective positions of Christianity and humanism in the history of western culture and at the present day. Very broadly speaking – and I would emphasize the broadness of the generalization – the classical world was essentially humanistic, this-worldly, in its thinking. Its emphasis was on man, on his dignity and potentiality. For Plato, man's aim was to attain to absolute Good — to God, if you like — but he was to do this by the use of his own rational powers. God was an ideal towards which man strove, but with no more direct role in man's destiny than this. Only in the "fringe" mystery religions, of which Christianity became one, was there a strong emphasis on supernatural powers, on powers above and beyond man, on which man in some way depended. In the medieval world, by contrast, the emphasis was on the supernatural, on man's need for help from God, for the "grace" of God, if he were to accomplish anything. The doctrine of original sin, as developed by Saint Paul and Saint Augustine, made of man a "miserable worm", incapable of anything unless aided by God. Life in this world was of no importance except as a preparation for the next.

The Renaissance, with its renewal of interest in everything classical, attempted a balance between these two attitudes. Ralph Waldo Emerson, the American philosopher, defined religion as "a set of obligations originating with God", and contrasted it with ethics, "a set of obligations originating with man". In this sense the attempt of the Renaissance was to balance the respective claims of religion and ethics: to balance man's responsibility to himself, his sense of his own worth and dignity, with his responsibility to God, his sense of his own inadequacy without the gift of God's grace. The attempt was by its nature doomed to failure, for man cannot believe absolutely in himself and at the same time believe in God. The most that religion can concede in the direction of humanism is a belief in man as made in God's image, and ultimately a choice has to be made. The inevitable failure of the Renaissance attempt is, I think, to be seen in subsequent developments. Humanism itself has gone on to become essentially an anti-religious movement; the battle in the USA for a completely secular education, for instance, has been led by the humanists. At the same time religion in its more traditional forms has become increasingly humanistic, increasingly concerned with man's welfare in this world, rather than with his preparation for the next, with his mortal body as much as with his immortal soul; while simultaneously new religious movements have developed which emphasize the supernatural element and seek to preach withdrawal from worldly concerns.

These generalizations are, as I have said, very broad — too broad, in fact, to be particularly meaningful. I use them simply in order to define the essential issues involved in Christian humanism, to make clear the conflicts and tensions involved in it, the imaginative potentialities of which lie behind the greatness not only of *Paradise Lost* but of much other Renaissance literature as well. One of the great problems that man has faced and always will face — perhaps, indeed, the greatest problem of all — is whether to believe finally in himself, in his ultimate need and ability to control his own destiny; or to see this destiny as in the end in the hands of some power outside himself, beyond his control. *Paradise Lost* is, I believe, at the very centre of this problem, and it is for this reason that it remains of vital interest.

I am suggesting then that *Paradise Lost* can be read as using the Christian story of the fall of man as a structure for an exploration of the choice which faces all men between a belief in themselves, in the primacy of their own human nature, and a belief in God; that is, as an image of the human dilemma, caught as man is between responsibility to himself and to God. I would stress, however, that I am saying only that it *can* be read in this way, and that to some extent this is the way I shall be reading it in the essays that follow; not that it *must* be read in this way, or even that I shall be exclusively seeking to fit it to this formula. Again, for reasons that I have already outlined, in saying this I am not suggesting that Milton necessarily set out to create this particular image; rather I would seek only to claim that it is an image of the human condition the potentiality for which manifestly lay within the seventeenth-century concept of Christian humanism, just as the potentiality for the modern meaning of *pandemonium* lay within Milton's original use of the word.

On the matter of Milton's conscious intentions, it would be dangerous to go further than to suggest that he set out to write an epic on the subject of man's fall and redemption. In doing this, however, he would feel the need to "amplify" the story, to add to it, to expand it in order to give it what Renaissance critics called verisimilitude, the appearance of truth, and to give it epic proportions. This is not to say that Milton was not himself convinced of the truth of the Christian story; rather that being convinced himself he sought to convince others of its truth by using the imaginative resources of poetry to embellish it. There is no doubt that in telling the story Milton would have felt himself bound by the original Biblical account; and also by the development and interpretation of that account which by the seventeenth century had from innumerable sources become part of the Christian tradition. But on the one hand the story as told in the Book of Genesis was so much only the basis, the scaffolding of a story; and on the other centuries of interpretation had provided such a wealth of choices associated with it and hallowed by tradition. Thus Milton would have a good deal of freedom in developing the story without being untrue either to its origins or to the traditions surrounding it.

What is important is the kind of choices which Milton made from among the material available from the tradition for the amplification of the story, and the kind of emphases, the kind of imaginative colouring given to the story by his treatment of these choices. It is here, in the particular treatment given to the story, that forces at work in Milton's psyche, the forces of Renaissance humanism, have, I believe, led the poem towards that image of the human dilemma that I have outlined. It is not necessary to see Milton himself as fully aware of these forces: indeed, it is perhaps only from the vantage point of the subsequent resolution to some extent of the Christian/humanist dichotomy that the processes at work in the poem are able to be recognized. In this sense, and to this extent, it may be as William Blake wrote in his *Marriage of Heaven and Hell* that Milton was "of the Devil's party without knowing it"; or to an extent even as William Empson claims that Milton is actually condemning God while professing to justify Him. But these questions of Milton's purpose, conscious or unconscious, are ultimately irrelevant. What Milton claims to be doing and what he actually does may seem sometimes to be differing, even opposing things; but whether this is a conscious device or an unconscious accident does not matter, except for what it reveals of Milton himself. What does matter is that this disparity is largely responsible for the enigmatic quality of the poem, and that this enigmatic quality is in part responsible for its continuing ability to attract and engross.

Paradise Lost then is Milton's version of the Eden myth. It reconstructs in epic form the events of man's creation, fall and promise of eventual redemption. But in the reconstruction the simple, distinct story of Adam and Eve, with its simple, distinct religious lesson of obedience to God, is injected with complexity. Moral and psychological issues of provocative importance are to be inferred from the narrative; and often these issues threaten to subvert the status of *Paradise Lost* as a Christian epic. There is often a turbulent tension between the straightforward story and its suggested or implied significance. Milton's professed aim for the poem is that it "justify the ways of God to men" (I. 26); that it should clarify the cause, the nature and the consequences of the fall first of Eve and then of Adam. But when the poem is read with more than superficial attention it seems often to challenge rather than to justify, to confuse rather than to clarify, to ask questions rather than to answer them. It is infuriating but also exciting for its elusive meanings. "Full of doubt I stand" Adam says to Michael towards the poem's end, as the vision of the future has been opened to him,

> Whether I should repent me now of sin
> By me done and occasioned, or rejoice
> Much more, that much more good thereof shall spring   (XII, 474–76)

Here it may be that Adam is simply expressing the concept that had become known in the Christian tradition as the "paradox of the fortunate fall", the belief that God's providence will ensure that from evil must come a good greater than any that has been destroyed. But Adam's doubt may seem to go further than this, and seem to be shared by Milton himself. At the beginning of the poem he begs of his muse, the Holy Spirit,

> . . . what in me is dark
> Illumine, what is low raise and support;

That to the highth of this great argument
I may assert eternal providence.   (I, 22–25)

Sometimes it may seem that Milton's muse has let him down, has offered him inspiration without sufficient explanation. He calls his poem a "great argument", but in many ways it may seem to be more a great exploration, an exploration for himself as much as for his readers.

Of the eight chapters that follow, the first is concerned as it were to set the stage, to show how man stands always at the centre of the poem, how Milton's real concern is always truly with man, with the human condition, rather than with God, devils or angels. And because of its nature this first chapter will also serve as a convenient introduction, providing a useful overview of the poem as a basis for those that follow. The next two chapters, dealing respectively with evil and freedom, aim to define these two vitally important terms around which much of the meaning of the poem revolves.

Then in the fourth chapter attention is turned to perhaps the most interesting of the poem's cast of characters, Eve, and her role in the story. The next subject is the puzzling account of the war in Heaven given to Adam by Raphael, and how its meaning for the fall of man may be interpreted. Then in the central chapter of the work we turn to the fall itself, in a search for a resolution of the contradictions and paradoxes of the poem, for a means of interpreting its stated aim of justifying the ways of God to men. Following this we look at the various patterns of tragedy in literature in relation to *Paradise Lost,* and suggest a particular form of tragedy which may be of special interest for an interpretation of the poem. And just as the first of the chapters may serve to set the stage, this one should help to bring together some of the matters already discussed, within one or other of the various patterns of tragedy. Finally we go to *Paradise Regained,* which in a sense is a sequel to *Paradise Lost* and in which Milton made his ultimate and, it will be suggested, unsuccessful attempt to fuse the claims of Christianity and humanism.

2

Man the Measure of All Things

Being an epic, *Paradise Lost* properly begins by stating its argument, by making clear what it is about:

> Of man's first disobedience, and the fruit
> Of that forbidden tree . . .   (I, 1–2)

Man is at once established at the centre of interest, and he remains there throughout the poem. I would begin by trying to give some idea of how the structure, the architecture of the poem, retains man in this central position.

The structure of *Paradise Lost* is basically spatial. Its movement takes place in space rather than in time. And again in keeping with its epic proportions, this space is enormous, including as it does the whole of space, metaphysical, as well as physical – our physical universe and the metaphysical universe of Heaven, Hell and Chaos which lie beyond it and which for the imaginative purposes of the poem are treated as if they too had the properties of physical space.

In the beginning – though immediately we are in difficulty because there is of course no beginning, just as there are, strictly speaking, no limits to the poem's space – at some time then, before the events with which the poem is concerned, there was only God. Following a clue given us incidentally during God's directions to the Son which resulted in the creation of our physical universe, we learn that God had chosen to withdraw, as it were, from part of Himself:

> . . . I am who fill
> Infinitude, nor vacuous the space,
> Though I uncircumscribed my self retire,
> And put not forth my goodness, which is free
> To act or not . . .   (VII, 168–72)

The result of this act was the division of the space of the poem into Heaven above and Chaos below, into God and non-God. Next must have come the creation by the Son, as the Word of God, of the angelic host which peoples Heaven, and of which again we learn only incidentally in the course of an argument between Satan and Abdiel at the time of Satan's rebellion against God. Abdiel chides Satan with wishing to set himself up

Equal to him begotten Son, by whom
As by his Word the mighty Father made
All things, even thee, and all the spirits of heaven.   (V, 835—37)

The creation of the Son himself, as distinct from the Father, is a matter on which Milton is careful to keep clear of controversy or heresy, if the invocation to Light at the beginning of Book III is indeed addressed to the Son:

Hail, holy Light, offspring of heaven first-born,
Or of the Eternal co-eternal beam
May I express thee unblamed . . .   (III, 1—3)

Typically in *Paradise Lost* (unlike, for instance, his *On Christian Doctrine*) Milton seems to prefer to keep away from theological problems, presumably because they might draw attention away from his poetic purpose. But whichever of these alternatives regarding the Son's creation is correct, the first event with which the poem is directly concerned is the exaltation of the Son to a position next to God, and the rebellion of Satan which follows from it. This rebellion results in the creation first of Hell as the place of punishment to which the fallen angels condemn themselves by their act of disobedience, and then of our physical universe, reclaimed from Chaos by the Son and hanging by a golden chain like a great ball from the floor of Heaven. This then is Milton's cosmos, with Heaven above, Hell below and Earth somewhere between, in the midst of Chaos. Any attempt to determine the magnitude or proportions of this cosmos such as some critics have attempted is, of course, impossible and irrelevant. For the space outside our own universe is not physical but metaphysical; moral or spiritual space, imagined as physical only in order to help our human understanding to some grasp of the events that take place there.

The actual physical universe of *Paradise Lost* is the Ptolemaic one, with Earth as a solid ball in the middle, surrounded, like a series of transparent balloons of increasing size, by the spheres that control the movement of the moon, the planets, the fixed stars and the sun, the whole system being kept spinning by a further sphere, the *primum mobile*, and with finally an outer adamantine sphere which protects it from the inroads of Chaos. There is more to it than this — an opening leading down from the uppermost point through the spheres to the earth, for instance — but the detail is largely unimportant for the poem. Two things, however, are important. Earth is placed at the centre of the system, and at the very centre of it there will be a "still point", around which all else is revolving. This "still centre of the turning world", to borrow an image from T. S. Eliot's *Four Quartets*, can without too great an imaginative effort be equated with the Garden, and specifically with the wedding bower of Adam and Eve — though logically, of course this is not so. One can readily believe that it was this central position of the earth that led Milton to adopt, for imaginative, aesthetic purposes, the Ptolemaic astronomical system, even though he certainly knew of the Copernican theory and had very likely visited Galileo in Italy and looked through his telescope. Indeed he mentions the "Tuscan artist" and his "optic glass", and has Raphael suggest to Adam that the Sun and not the earth may be "centre to the world", and the earth "so steadfast though she seem / Insensibly three different motions move" (VIII, 123—30). Clearly it is imaginatively preferable for man as the centre of interest to be located firmly at the centre rather than following a "wandering course now high, now low, then hid, / Progressive, retrograde, or standing still" (VIII, 126—7). The same reason may be seen, too, for Milton's having placed Hell at the bottom of the whole cosmos and not as more traditionally — in Dante's *Inferno,* for instance — somewhere beneath the surface of the earth itself, in which case Hell, and not the Garden, would have been the "still centre". It would also have retained Hell within the physical universe, rather than as part of the metaphysical space beyond, where it belongs. Ultimately evil is a moral, not a physical, phenomenon.

This then is the stage on which the first ten books of *Paradise Lost* are enacted, and it remains to be seen how the action is fitted into the space it provides. We might begin with the image of God's golden compasses, used by the Son to mark out the limits of the physical universe from Chaos at its creation:

> . . . in his hand
> He took the golden compasses, prepared
> In God's eternal store, to circumscribe
> This universe, and all created things:
> One foot he centred, and the other turned
> Round through the vast profundity obscure. (VII, 224—29)

At the beginning of the creation of his epic, we can see Milton, like the Son, place the fixed foot at the centre, on man, and then with the moving foot mark in the outer limits of Heaven and Hell. "Say first" he demands of his "muse", the Holy Spirit, "for heaven hides nothing from thy view / Nor the deep tract of hell"; then from Hell he draws the moving foot across the centre with a reference to the fall — "what cause / Moved our grand parents . . . / . . . to fall off / From their creator" — back to Heaven with a brief reference to "The infernal serpent . . . what time his pride / Had cast him out from heaven, with all his host" (I, 27—37). Finally as the rebellious angels are

> Hurled headlong flaming down from th'ethereal sky,
> With hideous ruin and combustion down
> To bottomless perdition . . .   (I, 45—47)

the moving foot swings back to Hell, where it is to remain for a time as the story begins – though not at the beginning, but in the manner of epic in the midst of things.

For most of the first two books the scene of action is in Hell, but it is not very long before attention is turned upwards towards the earth and man. The fallen angels themselves are introduced not so much in their role as such but as those who "wandering o'er the earth" among "the sons of Eve / Got them new names" (I, 364–65). There follows a roll call of pagan gods and demons, including the travesty of Christ's disciples in the twelve "disciples" – Moloch, Baal, Ashtoreth and so on – whom Milton has gathered around Satan. The point of this reference to events yet to come on earth becomes apparent as Satan speaks of the newly created world, and suggests that "Thither, if but to pry, shall be perhaps / Our first eruption" (I, 655–6). Our world has already become closely associated with the denizens of Hell, is already imaginatively swarming with them. And the rest of Book I and the beginning of Book II are a carefully stage-managed preparation for Satan's assault on Adam and Eve. By the end of Book II Satan has left Hell and journeying up through Chaos has come within sight of "this pendent world". The movement of the poem towards the centre, towards its ultimate destination in the mind of man, has begun.

With the invocation to Light at the beginning of Book III, we leave Satan for the time being and continue upwards to Heaven, to the debate between the Father and the Son which parallels the Council held earlier in Hell. But here again, though the scene is at the outer limits of the poem's cosmos, our attention is directed downwards, towards the earth, first as the speakers watch Satan moving towards it through Chaos and later as they discuss the consequences for man of Satan's incursion into the Garden. Then towards the end of the book we return to Satan and travel with him down through the spheres of the physical universe until "on Niphates' top he lights" (III, 742). Thus the inward pressure of the narrative is maintained; and it is continued on into the fourth book as Satan approaches Eden, until finally we enter the Garden with him, and with him catch our first glimpse of those who "in their looks divine / The image of their glorious maker shone" (IV, 291–92). Throughout most of the remainder of the Book IV we watch and listen to Adam and Eve as they move towards their wedding bower, until

> Thus talking hand in hand alone they passed
> On to their blissful bower . . .   (IV, 689–90)

We have now indeed reached the "still centre of the turning world".

With Book V the Archangel Raphael arrives in the Garden, sent by God to warn Adam and Eve of their danger. His narrative turns eventually to the war in Heaven, and now our perspective has changed. Now that we have reached the centre we stand there looking outwards, towards events on the periphery, instead of looking inwards towards the earth. With the end of Raphael's account of the war in Heaven, which takes us through Book VI, and with a brief reminder of Hell at the end of the book, the second inward movement beings, as Raphael goes on to describe the creation by the Son of the physical universe. We have in fact now largely finished with events beyond the earth, and are ready to "Descend from heaven", though

> Half yet remains unsung, but narrower bound
> Within the visible diurnal sphere;
> Standing on earth, not rapt above the pole.   (VII, 21–23)

And the concentration on earthly things is continued as Adam tells Raphael in Book VIII of his own and Eve's creation.

At the beginning of Book IX the climax of the poem is approaching, the fall itself, which simultaneously completes the inward movement and begins the reversing, outward movement. As he determines to follow Eve in eating the apple, Adam – as Eve had done before him – "First to himself he inward silence broke" (IX, 895). The fall is something which takes place right at the centre, within the very mind of man. And it is in the mind of man that its immediate effects are felt, in feelings of lust, then of shame, anger, impotence, directed by Adam and Eve first towards themselves and then toward each other. At the same time, prefigured indeed by the parting of Adam and Eve before the actual fall, the effects of the fall spread out like a stain, first through the Garden as the animals, which had hitherto lived in peace, begin to attack each other, and then beyond it to the rest of the cosmos. This spreading of the effects of the fall through the physical and moral space of the poem continues to occupy it through the rest of Book IX and most of Book X, until at the end of the latter the very first signs of the redemption promised in Book III are seen: a new phase, in which the movement will not only be centred on man but, as he strives to attain the "paradise within", wholly contained within him, has begun. The spatial movement of the poem with man as its constant centre is now complete.

Books XI and XII return to the form and movement of V and VI – Raphael's account of the war in Heaven – except that, instead of looking out from the centre to events taking place in space, our perspective is now one of time. First in a series of visions and then as he listens to the Archangel Michael's narrative, Adam looks out from the Garden into the future history of the human race, revealed with increasing speed until it reaches the time of the last judgement,

> When this world's dissolution shall be ripe.   (XII, 459)

Just as in the first ten books the epic magnitude of the poem had encompassed the whole of space, in the last two the whole of human time is included. And the poem ends with a return to Adam and Eve once again hand in hand as when we first saw them, but this time, instead of moving inwards towards their wedding bower, towards the still centre, they are moving outwards towards the unknown:

> The world was all before them, where to choose
> Their place of rest, and providence their guide:
> They hand in hand with wandering steps and slow,
> Through Eden took their solitary way.   (XII, 646—49)

The "architecture" of the poem, and there is no doubt that it is a masterly architecture, keeps man then securely at its centre. And there are other important ways, as well as minor ones, in which the humanistic emphasis of the poem is maintained. We might look, as an example, at the treatment of Hell in the opening books. The initial picture is one that would be familiar, in its general outline, from Dante's *Inferno* and many other medieval descriptions and illustrations:

> A dungeon horrible, on all sides round
> As one great furnace flamed, yet from those flames
> No light, but rather darkness visible
> Served only to discover sights of woe,
> Regions of sorrow, doleful shades, where peace
> And rest can never dwell, hope never comes
> That comes to all; but torture without end
> Still urges, and a fiery deluge, fed
> With ever-burning sulphur unconsumed.   (I, 61—69)

But this initially conventional description seems only to serve as an intro-duction by way of the known, or expected; and thereafter what landscape painting there is, though desolate enough, seems more like a picture of the bleaker parts of the world than our usual notions of Hell. After Satan has left on his journey up through Chaos, some of his companions set out to explore their new domain, and

> On bold adventure to discover wide
> That dismal world, if any clime perhaps
> Might yield them easier habitation, bend
> Four ways their flying march, along the banks
> Of four infernal rivers that disgorge
> Into the burning lake their baleful streams;
> Abhorred Styx the flood of deadly hate,
> Sad Acheron . . .
> Beyond this flood a frozen continent
> Lies dark and wild, beat with perpetual storms
> Of whirlwind and dire hail, which on firm land
> Thaws not, but gathers heap, and ruin seems
> Of ancient pile; all else deep snow and ice,
> A gulf profound . . .   (II, 571—92)

The familiar names are here, and their associations, but the picture is less one of Hell than of the more hellish regions of the earth. And the same is true of its inhabitants. Though they bear the names of pagan gods and demons, their behaviour and their speeches are distinctively human, and the picture that builds up seems more like Milton's vision, not of Hell, but again of the more hellish aspects of seventeenth-century England.

Milton's Hell is not a place of disorder — quite the contrary: though unlike Heaven, where order is spontaneous, it is an imposed, military order. No sooner are the fallen angels clear of the burning lake into which they originally fell than they form up in military array:

> All in a moment through the gloom were seen
> Ten thousand banners rise into the air,
> With orient colours waving . . .
> . . . Anon they move
> In perfect phalanx to the Dorian mood
> Of flutes and soft recorders; such as raised
> To highth of noblest temper heroes old
> Arming to battle, and in stead of rage
> Deliberate valour breathed, firm and unmoved
> With dread of death to flight or foul retreat.   (I, 544—55)

It is a military parade of a kind with which the twentieth century is only too familiar; and those who have seen films of the Nuremburg rallies of the 1930s will recognize the figure of Satan as he appears before his followers:

> . . . Darkened so, yet shone
> Above them all the archangel: but his face
> Deep scars of thunder had intrenched, and care
> Sat on his faded cheek, but under brows
> Of dauntless courage, and considerate pride
> Waiting revenge; cruel his eye, but cast
> Signs of remorse and passion . . .
> Thrice he essayed, and thrice in spite of scorn,
> Tears such as angels weep, burst forth: at last
> Words interwove with sighs found out their way.   (I, 599—621)

It is impossible not to feel the irony of this, particularly as the events which follow from it are carefully stage-managed as by a consummate politician. The immediate response to his rhetoric is predictable:

> He spake: and to confirm his words, out flew
> Millions of flaming swords, drawn from the thighs
> Of mighty cherubim . . .
> Hurling defiance toward the vault of heaven   (I, 663—69)

But before Satan's plan can be put into effect, Pandemonium, the great meeting place of the devils, must be built. The materials are near at hand:

> There stood a hill not far whose grisly top
> Belched fire and rolling smoke; the rest entire
> Shone with a glossy scurf, undoubted sign
> That in his womb was hid metallic ore,
> The work of sulphur. Thither winged with speed
> A numerous brigade hastened . . .
> Opened into the hill a spacious wound
> And digged out ribs of gold . . .   (I, 670–90)

The earthly parallel is clear enough, for the twentieth century even more perhaps than the seventeenth, but Milton insists on it:

> . . . Mammon led them on,
> Mammon, the least erected spirit that fell
> From heaven . . .
> . . . by him first
> Men also, and by his suggestion taught,
> Ransacked the centre, and with impious hands
> Rifled the bowels of their mother earth
> For treasures better hid . . .   (I, 678–88)

It is not difficult to imagine where Milton would have stood in some of the present-day conservationist controversies!

However it is in the conduct of the Council itself that the reader is most likely to feel the parallel with earthly affairs. It is participatory democracy, but in order to fit the multitude into the council chambers,

> Behold a wonder! they but now who seemed
> In bigness to surpass Earth's giant sons,
> Now less than smallest dwarfs, in narrow room
> Throng numberless . . .   (I, 777–80)

Not so their leaders:

> . . . But far within
> And in their own dimensions like themselves,
> The great seraphic lords and cherubim
> In close recess and secret conclave sat,
> A thousand demi-gods on golden seats
> Frequent and full . . .   (I, 792–97)

Is it perhaps the infamous Court of Star Chamber that Milton has in mind?

Under the eye of Satan in all his splendour, the "delegates" have their say, in speeches which have all the hallmarks of political rhetoric. But it is clear that even this is only for the sake of appearances. When they have made their proposals, Satan's lieutenant Beelzebub rises on cue to propose a scheme "first devised / By Satan, and in part proposed" (II, 379–80). The scheme – to invade the newly created Earth – is carried by acclamation, and Beelzebub asks who will undertake the dangerous mission. "But all sat mute", and the stage is set for Satan to take on, with a maximum of

glory for himself, what he had already determined to do. And he is careful
to ensure that he will have all the glory:

> ... this enterprise
> None shall partake with me. Thus saying rose
> The monarch, and prevented all reply,
> Prudent, lest from his resolution raised
> Others among the chief might offer now
> (Certain to be refused) what erst they feared;
> And so refused might in opinion stand
> His rivals, winning cheap the high repute
> Which he through hazard huge must earn ...   (II, 465–73)

Again Milton makes clear the parallel with the conduct of men, this time a
parallel made double edged by irony. The hellish multitude extol their
leader,

> That for the general safety he despised
> His own: for neither do the spirits damned
> Lose all their virtue; lest bad men should boast
> Their specious deeds on earth, which glory excites,
> Or close ambition varnished o'er with zeal.   (II, 481–85)

Satan departs, and his companions occupy themselves in the familiar ways
of the world — in martial games, music, philosophical discussion, exploration — as "each his several way / Pursues ... where he may likeliest find /
Truce to his restless thoughts" (II, 523–26). A Miltonic comment perhaps
on the use made by man of his leisure time.

Hell then comes to look increasingly like Earth, like the "fallen" world,
the world with which the reader is only too familiar. It is for this reason,
perhaps, that these two books have been often thought of as the most
successful in the poem. But the earthly frame of reference is of more
importance than simply giving the poem greater dramatic immediacy. In
the image of the human condition presented by *Paradise Lost* Satan and
Hell are not things beyond the bounds of human life. They represent
rather one of the poles of a continuum, Christ and Heaven being of course
the other, with unfallen man at the centre but able by his own actions to
move in either direction: upwards towards Christ or downwards towards
Satan. Although, as we shall find in later essays, we cannot be certain that
the image is ultimately as simple as it is stated here to be; that the choice
between good and evil, between the way of Christ and the way of Satan,
is an entirely straightforward one.

The human reference of the portrayal of Satan is continued and
developed in the fourth book, in the great dramatic soliloquy which
Milton had first written many years before the composition of *Paradise
Lost*, as the opening speech of a classical style drama on the subject of the
Genesis story. In the first two books Satan has appeared as a martial hero

whose self-seeking desire for glory is none the less exposed. In this soliloquy, and in others which follow, he appears as an even more directly human figure, a man with still some instinct for good, for pity and remorse, but one so firmly in the grip of his own ambition, his self-pride, his need for adulation, that he is no longer able to respond to it; so that when God in the previous book had declared that Satan would not "find grace" He was in a sense simply recognizing a psychological fact. Satan is man beyond redemption, though still recognizably man. As he watches and listens to Adam and Eve he speaks to himself, and as we overhear him we follow the workings of the mind, not of a devil, but of an evil man:

> Sight hateful, sight tormenting! Thus these two
> Imparadised in one another's arms
> . . . while I to hell am thrust.
>
> .   .   .   .   .
> You let me not forget what I have gained
> From their own mouths; all is not theirs it seems;
> One fatal tree there stands of knowledge called,
> Forbidden them to taste: knowledge forbidden?
> Suspicious, reasonless! Why should their Lord
> Envy them that? . . .
> . . . is that their happy state,
> The proof of their obedience and their faith?
> O fair foundation laid whereon to build
> Their ruin! Hence I will excite their minds
> With more desire to know, and to reject
> Envious commands, invented with design
> To keep them low whom knowledge might exalt
> Equal with gods. Aspiring to be such,
> They taste and die . . .   (IV, 505–27)

Notice how as he goes on Satan thinks his way, as it were, into the minds of his intended victims.

There is no doubt that the two most successful characters in *Paradise Lost* are Satan and Eve and they are also the two most fully developed in human terms. On the other hand, the opposite end of the scale of human potentiality from Satan and Hell — Christ and Heaven — is relatively unsuccessful, largely because its human reference is less fully developed; indeed probably because it lacks the potentiality for such development. God the Father gains some human quality from the derisory, satiric elements in his make-up, deriving from the Old Testament tradition. But the Son, at least in *Paradise Lost – Paradise Regained* is a different matter, to be explored elsewhere — remains a largely colourless creation, an abstract presentation of the qualities of love and mercy. Among the inhabitants of Heaven who remain faithful it is the lesser lights who are the most dramatically alive, and this in proportion to their seeming humanity; Abdiel, for instance, in his passionately wordy battles with

Satan before and during the war in Heaven. And the Archangels Raphael and Gabriel, the first the "sociable" angel with his not always entirely infallible information and his gallantry towards Adam and Eve, and the latter particularly in his encounter with Satan after the latter's first incursion into the Garden.

This meeting between Satan and Gabriel, indeed, is one of the great minor scenes of the poem, and despite its fantastic nature is only too human. Satan has been discovered by Gabriel's messengers "Squat like a toad, close at the ear of Eve" (IV, 800), and after startling his captors by his sudden rematerialization is haled off to confront Gabriel. There follows a war of words in which the two strive to outdo each other in insulting titles — "proud limitary Cherum", "insulting angel" and so on — until, as the narrator says "dreadful deeds might have ensured", although it seems fairly clear that they would not have done. We can rather feel each taking a step backwards with each successive insult. However,

> The eternal to prevent such horrid fray,
> Hung forth in heaven his golden scales . . .   (IV, 996—97)

The meaning of the scales, and the fact that one side goes up and the other down, seem quite enigmatic (despite the commentators' attempts at explanation). But Satan's guilty conscience is enough to interpret their meaning for him:

> . . . The fiend looked up and knew
> His mounted scale aloft: nor more; but fled
> Murmuring, and with him fled the shades of night.   (IV, 1013—15)

It is possible, indeed to an extent necessary, to see Satan as the personification of evil: just, as will be discussed elsewhere, Adam and Eve may, to an extent, be seen as personifications of certain aspects of the human psyche. But none of the three could, in the full context of the poem, be described as allegorical or symbolic figures. Though he is at times painted as larger than life, our response to Satan remains that to a man wholly given over to evil, rather than a response to abstract evil. There are occasions, however, when Milton does launch into overt allegory — in the Sin and Death episodes, in the portrayal of "Chaos and Old Night" and in the account of Satan's return to Hell after the fall — and then, I think, the poem is less successful. Not because the episodes are necessarily bad allegory — though one of them, Satan's meeting with Chaos and Night is, I believe, bad or at least inconsistent allegory — but because such episodes do not fit into the basically human frame of reference of the poem. In so far as they do so fit, indeed, they are successful. Satan's meeting with Sin at the gates of Hell, for instance, achieves a fine dramatic quality which enables us to forget Sin's purely allegorical existence, except when this is insisted on in the details of her appearance and her origin.

Milton is, of course, dealing with many things which may be seen as lying beyond the scope of human understanding, and the Christian tradition provided him with what was known as the doctrine of accommodation, whereby these things could be related in such a way as to "accomodate" them to our limited intelligence. Thus when Adam calls on Raphael to tell him about Satan's rebellion and the events which led up to the creation of the world, Raphael answers:

> High matter thou enjoinest me, O prime of men,
> Sad task and hard, for how shall I relate
> To human sense the invisible exploits
> Of warring spirits . . .
> . . . what surmounts the reach
> Of human sense, I shall delineate so,
> By likening spiritual to corporeal forms,
> As may express them best . . .   (V, 563—74)

But then he goes on to suggest "what if earth / Be but the shadow of heaven, and things therein / Each to other like, more than on earth is thought?". And as we shall see in a later essay, the war in Heaven, like events in Hell, does indeed have some close resemblances to what goes on in our own world.

There are other occasions, too, when Raphael is at pains to lessen the gap between man and the angels; when, for instance, as part of his exposition of the "great chain of being" he differentiates between human and angelic understanding. Fancy and understanding, he says, are the source whence the soul

> Reason receives, and reason is her being,
> Discursive or intuitive: discourse
> Is oftest yours, the latter most is ours,
> Differing but in degree, of kind the same.   (V, 487—90)

The difference is one of degree, not of kind, and "time may come when men / With angels may participate" (V, 493—94). Elsewhere Raphael is led to discourse on the angelic digestion and, in answer to a question from Adam on angelic love-making, with a suggestion even of an angelic blush:

> . . . Let it suffice thee that thou know'st
> Us happy . . .
> . . . If spirits embrace
> Total they mix, union of pure with pure
> Desiring, nor restrained conveyance need
> As flesh to mix with flesh, or soul with soul.   (VIII, 620—29)

These passages have provided critics with some opportunity for merriment at Milton's expense, but their purpose is clear. The less wide the gap between man and the angels the easier it is to see the reference for man of events which take place outside his own universe, to keep man at the centre of interest.

As this human reference continues to hold, the cosmological image begins to change. In place of a physical universe of man, separated by its outer adamantine sphere from the metaphysical space that lies beyond it, we are increasingly made conscious of a physical universe in which the overt events of the narrative are played out by human and human-seeming characters, and a psychological, moral universe, which more and more appears as the true scene of action, and which lies not somewhere outside the physical universe but at its very centre, in the mind of man — even to the extent, if one wishes to take the step, of seeing Satan himself as no more than the outward symbol of forces at work within man. Man is not, as he appeared in the opening lines, simply at the centre of the stage; in the combination of his moral and physical life he finally is the stage.

In so far as this is true, it is ironic that Milton, on the ground that he "pursues / Things unattempted yet in prose or rhyme" (I, 15–16), things beyond the reach of human understanding, should take on himself the mantle of the blind poet-prophet, should call on the Holy Spirit to "aid my adventurous song". For the answer he was seeking lay not in the outermost reaches of metaphysical space but within himself, within his own experience of the human condition. And the poem continues to attract readers because it speaks as well to their human experience and understanding.

3

Yet Evil Whence?

What is evil, and where does it come from? This is a question that has always been at the forefront of Christian theorizing. Put simply, the problem is this: if the world and everything in it was created by God, as Christianity has always claimed, then if evil exists it too must have been part of God's creation. Saint Augustine had asked this question before the end of the fourth century:

> How, then, do I come to possess a will that can choose to do wrong and refuse to do good, thereby providing a just reason why I should be punished? Who put this will into me? Who sowed this seed of bitterness in me, when all that I am was made by my God, who is sweetness itself? If it was the devil who put it there, who made the devil? If he was a good angel who became a devil because of his wicked will, how did he come to possess the wicked will which made him a devil, when the Creator, who is entirely good, made him a good angel and nothing else?[1]

Answers up to Milton's time had been mainly of two kinds. Firstly, what appears to be evil only *seems* to be so because our understanding is partial. We see only part of the truth, part of the whole, in which everything, apparent evil included, is directed by God's providence towards an ultimate good end. "All partial evil, universal good" as Alexander Pope declared in that compendium of Renaissance commonplaces, the First Epistle of *The Essay on Man,* with its triumphant conclusion, "Whatever is, is Right". And secondly, not incompatible with this, concerned with the origin rather than the nature of evil, evil is denied any positive existence; rather it is negative, created not by God, but by the denial or rejection of God. As Saint Augustine concluded, "when I asked myself what wickedness was, I saw that it was not a substance but perversion of the will when it turns aside from you". These two views of evil had long existed side by side in the Christian tradition, as they do in *Paradise Lost.*

To take the second of these beliefs first, the essentially negative nature of evil. In the great cosmos created by Milton as a stage for his epic narrative, prior to the first overt emergence of evil in Satan's rebellion against the elevation of the Son to a position next to God, "being" consisted of

1. Saint Augustine, *Confessions,* trans. R. S. Price-Coffin, Penguin Classics, pp. 136–37.

Heaven above and Chaos below. Chaos is that part of Himself from which God had voluntarily withdrawn. It is not evil; it may appear to be allied to evil in the account of Satan's journey through it on his way to attack Earth, but this is, I think, an inconsistency in the narrative. It is not evil, but is simply a lack of the order characteristic of Heaven, not a specific rejection of it. It results from a withdrawal *by* God, not a withdrawal *from* God. Hell on the other hand, which *is* evil, is created by Satan's act of rebellion against God.

The first we hear of Hell is in Raphael's account of the war in Heaven, when he reports God's direction to the Archangel Michael to

> . . . lead forth to battle these my sons
> Invincible . . .
> . . . them with fire and hostile arms
> Fearless assault, and to the brow of Heaven
> Pursuing drive them out from God and bliss
> Into their place of punishment, the gulf
> Of Tartarus, which ready opens wide
> His fiery chaos to receive their fall.   (VI, 46—55)

Hell, it would seem, has already been created by Satan's act, and when they meet later in the battle Michael greets him as

> Author of evil, unknown till thy revolt,
> Unnamed in heaven, now plenteous, as thou seest
> These acts of hateful strife . . .
> . . . how has thou disturbed
> Heaven's blessed peace, and into nature brought
> Misery, uncreated till the crime
> Of thy rebellion . . .   (VI, 262—69)

For Satan at this time Hell is indeed unknown, no more than a "fable", and ironically he underlines his part in the creation of evil by threatening to " . . . turn this heaven it self into the hell / Thou fablest . . . " (VI, 291—92), a threat which is recognizably brought to fruition as the "celestial soil" of Heaven is despoiled to gain the materials for gunpowder and cannon balls, and as the combatants

> . . . the neighbouring hills uptore:
> So hills amid the air encountered hills
> Hurled to and fro with jaculation dire,
> That under ground they fought in dismal shade.   (VI, 663—66)

This brings Hell itself to mind, and also serves to deepen the irony of Satan's proud-sounding boast after his arrival there — which we, of course, have already heard — to make "A heaven of hell, a hell of heaven" (I, 255). What Satan does not realize is that the first part of this boast is now beyond his power, while the second is for him now so much a certainty as to be no longer a matter of choice. By his rejection of God he has indeed made a Hell for himself, whether it be in Heaven, in Hell or anywhere else:

> Which way I fly is hell; myself am hell.   (IV, 75)

The other view of evil as partial, as part only of a wider good imposed by God's providence, is implied early in the poem and provides an ironic background for Satan's boasting. Seeing what is in fact now his inevitable doom, to create more and more evil, as being instead a matter of continuing choice, he claims that he will use his choice to defeat God's aims:

> . . . If then his providence
> Out of our evil seek to bring forth good,
> Our labour must be to pervert that end,
> And out of good still to find means of evil.   (I, 162–65)

What he does not understand is that this project is as futile as was his original act of rebellion, that God's providence cannot be circumvented. He has no choice, no real power, except in so far as

> . . . the will
> And high permission of all-ruling heaven
> Left him at large to his own dark designs,
> That with reiterated crimes he might
> Heap on himself damnation, while he sought
> Evil to others, and enraged might see
> How his malice served but to bring forth
> Infinite goodness, grace and mercy . . .   (I, 211–18)

Evil then is self-generating, but it is also eventually self-defeating. It stems from the ultimate, the original sin – the rejection of God – and all it can do of its own volition is to produce further evil. But paradoxically, while it seeks to create more evil it must inevitably by the operation of God's providence ultimately result in a good greater than any destroyed by it. These are the essential facts of evil as it is presented to us in *Paradise Lost*, and as such they are wholly traditional. Problems, however, remain, inherent in these apparently simple facts, and it is the imaginative development of these problems in the poem that offers a more difficult challenge to readers of *Paradise Lost* and that may seem to take us beyond the limits of traditional Christian theology.

By seeing evil as created not by God but by the evil doer's sin we are, of course, simply pushing the problem back a stage. If Satan created evil by his rejection of God – if evil did not in fact exist until he made that rejection – what was it that led him to make, or allowed him to make, this rejection, to choose his own way rather than the way of God. This, indeed, is the question that Saint Augustine had asked in the passage from his *Confessions* quoted earlier. "If it was the devil" he asks "who made the devil?" The answer must be that there was within the evil doer a potentiality for evil, for making the wrong choice; and in regard to the fallen angels this is explicit stated by God. "The first sort" he declares, referring to Satan and his followers, "by their own suggestion fell / Self-tempted, self-depraved" (III, 129—30). Their evil, in other words, is innate.

But there is a more positive side to it than this; it is not simply that the potentiality for making the wrong choice must be there, but that its existence is essential for what God declares to be the "nature of angels and of men", their freedom:

> I formed them free and free they must remain
> Till they enthrall themselves: I else must change
> Their nature, and revoke the high decree
> Unchangeable, eternal, which ordained
> Their freedom . . .   (III, 124—28)

Without the potentiality for making a wrong choice, without indeed a wrong choice to be made, there could be no freedom. Without any alternative, goodness would be a matter of necessity, which for God has no meaning:

> Freely they stood who stood, and fell who fell.
> Not free, what proof could they have given sincere
> Of true allegiance, constant faith or love,
> Where only what they needs must do appeared,
> Not what they would. . .   (III, 102—6)

God's justice towards his creatures, therefore, must include creating them with at least the potentiality for sin. He had me, He says of man, "All that he could have; I made him just and right, / Sufficient to have stood, though free to fall" (III, 98—99). And freedom to sin must include at least the potentiality for sin. Indeed, not only the potentiality apparently, but a potentiality equal in strength to its opposite, as God declared in asserting that no decree of His in any way interfered with man's free will, "to her own inclining left / In even scale" (X, 46—47).

In describing man as able to stand but free to fall if he chose, God is being more accurate, it would seem, than was Raphael in a statement that he made later to Adam, that "God made thee perfect, not immutable" (V, 524). It is clear that neither man nor angel was created perfect, otherwise neither could have fallen. Raphael's statement is contradictory. Man is indeed mutable and therefore not perfect; and this must be, for otherwise he would not be free, but locked, as it were, in his own perfection — as indeed is God. The choice is one between perfection and freedom, and for God in creating man the latter was to be preferred. For it must be remembered that in creating man God's purpose was ultimately to repopulate Heaven, out of Satan's rebellion to create

> Another world; out of one man a race
> Of men innumerable, there to dwell,

> Not here, till by degrees of merit raised,
> They open to themselves at length the way
> Up hither, under long obedience tried.   (VII, 155–59)

There must be room for improvement. By creating man sufficient to stand
yet still able to fall, God provides the conditions under which man will
have the opportunity to prove his "merit". He will be "under long
obedience tried", in circumstances where disobedience is always a possibility. And if this is God's way, it is also Milton's, as is made clear in a
passage from his treatise against censorship, *Areopagitica*, which despite
its fame is still worth quoting:

> . . . what wisdom can there be to choose, what continence to forebear,
> without the knowledge of evil? He that can apprehend and consider
> vice with all her baits and seeming pleasures, and yet abstain, and yet
> distinguish, and yet prefer that which is truly better, he is the true way-
> faring Christian. I cannot praise a fugitive and cloistered virtue, un-
> exercised and unbreathed, that never sallies out and sees her adversary,
> but slinks out of the race where that immortal garland is to be run for,
> not without dust and heat.[2]

The passage from *Areopagitica* is, of course, written from the point of
view of "fallen" man, man who lives in a world in which evil is an accomplished fact and who brings "not innocence into the world" but "impurity
much rather". But a great deal of the dramatic and imaginative force of
Paradise Lost works towards breaking down the barrier between fallen and
unfallen man; towards seeing the difference between the fallen and
unfallen worlds as resulting certainly from the fall, but the fall itself as
deriving from factors within man. Man, even unfallen man, brings "impurity" into the world, as a necessary condition of his freedom. Thus
when God, discussing future events with the Son as they watch Satan
making his way towards the earth, asserts that

> . . . man will hearken to his glozing lies,
> And easily transgress the sole command,
> Sole pledge of his obedience: so will fall,
> He and his faithless progeny. . . .   (III, 93–96)

it may be that He is simply displaying His omniscience. Or it may be that
He is stating an inescapable psychological fact: that being free to fall,
even though able to stand, it is virtually certain that man will fall. Which
is perhaps not difficult to accept, since by the terms of the "long
obedience" laid down by God man is in the position of the unfortunate
virgin who though she says "no" a thousand times need only say "yes"
once.

2. From *Areopagitica: A Speech for the Liberty of Unlicensed Printing, to the
   Parliament of England* (1644); quoted from Douglas Bush (ed.) *The Portable
   Milton*, p. 167.

If the seeds of the fall are in man's original nature, then at least the potentiality for evil is in the Garden from the beginning; and certainly we as readers never see it free of explicit evil, since we enter it and catch our first glimpse of Adam and Eve in company with Satan. This is examined in more detail in a later essay, particularly in relation to Eve's role in the story, but the parallel situation of Heaven before Satan's overt revolt provides a convenient illustration in the person of Mammon, described as

> . . . the least erected spirit that fell
> From heaven, for even in heaven his looks and thoughts
> Were always downwards bent, admiring more
> The riches of heaven's pavement, trodden gold,
> Than aught divine or holy else enjoyed
> In vision beatific . . .   (I, 679–84)

Apparently even in Heaven the tendency toward wrong did not have to await Satan's revolt. And this tendency to see evil as existing in embryo also in man's very nature gives point to the manner of Satan's entry into the Garden on two occasions. On the first of these, after viewing the difficulty of the closely guarded gate, "Due entrance he disdained, and in contempt, / At one slight bound high over leaped all bound" (IV, 180–81). The immediate significance of this, one that fits with Milton's attitude to censorship expressed in *Areopagitica,* is that it is useless to set up external barriers to evil. But it also suggests that the Garden is a place where evil may "come and go", as Adam, on the occasion of Eve's dream induced by Satan, suggests it may do "into the mind of god or man" (V, 117–19). On the second occasion of Satan's entering the Garden, just prior to the fall itself, he does so in a place where "Rose up a fountain by the tree of life; / . . . and with it rose / Satan . . . " (IX, 73–75). Here Satan rises at the foot of the tree of life, at the very source of life itself, despite the fact that this is still the "unfallen" world.

The Garden then, as the state of pre-fallen innocence, is not a place where evil has no part. What it is rather is a world in which there is evil, but one in which the will remains as yet untouched by evil. Evil, in other words, as Saint Augustine recognized, is an act of will. God could, had he wished, have maintained the outward purity of the Garden by holding Satan fast in Hell, a fact made clear by his ironic comments to the Son as they watch Satan making his way through Chaos towards Earth:

> Only begotten Son, seest thou what rage
> Transports our adversary, whom no bounds
> Prescribed, no bars of hell, nor all the chains
> Heaped on him there, nor yet the main abyss
> Wide interrupt, can hold; so bent he seems
> On desperate revenge . . .   (III, 80–85)

One wonders whether here Milton may be having God say in words which are *apparently* ironic but in fact not ironic at all, something which he (Milton) believed but would not want to say directly; something which is implicit throughout the poem — that evil is everywhere part of the scheme of things, before as after the fall, and not to be contained within any specific bounds. But to take the words at their face value — or rather simply at one ironic remove from their face value — God could, as I have said, have restrained Satan, but to have done so would have been to interfere with man's freedom by depriving him of the opportunity to prove his obedience; just as on another occasion Adam cannot act to save Eve from the consequences of her free choice. Man must, in God's own words, be "left to his own free will" (V, 236); and all that is needed from God, according to the narrator, for Him to have "fulfilled all justice" is to ensure that man be warned, "Lest wilfully transgressing he pretend / Surprisal, unadmonished, unforewarned" (V, 244—45). But not only this. Man's freedom not only demands that he be not artificially protected against evil; the very existence of evil is necessary in order to provide the essential condition for the exercise of that freedom and, by the continued right exercise of his freedom, for him to be able to earn eventually his place among the angels in Heaven.

To sum up then, evil in *Paradise Lost* is not simply part of the wider scheme of God's providence; it is an essential element in it, without which the basic condition of man's nature, his freedom, could not be fully realized. The implications of this for the poem's image of the human condition, and in particular of the fall, will be looked at in a later essay.

Various episodes in the poem serve to elaborate the image of evil. Hell, for instance, we are told is "Created evil, for evil only good" (II, 623). It is presented, at least in the beginning, as the traditional place of physical torment. However, we should remember that the spatial organization of *Paradise Lost* includes metaphysical as well as physical space, and that despite its physical image Hell is part of the former. Evil, as we have seen, is ultimately an inner, spiritual state of which, on this level, the physical Hell of the poem is an image, and its physical presentation provides a setting in which the moral quality and significance of the events which take place there can be judged. Of these events, the most important, or at least most extensive, is the great council meeting in Pandemonium, and it is interesting to look at the solutions to the plight in which the fallen angels find themselves offered by the first three speakers in the debate.

Moloch, the first speaker, is very much the rough soldier man. Not for him the refinements of diplomacy or the cunning of intrigue. His only answer is to hit back, irrespective of the consequences:

His trust was with the eternal to be deemed
Equal in strength, and rather than be less
Cared not to be at all; with that care lost
Went all his fear: of God, or hell, or worse.   (II, 46—49)

He is followed in the debate by Belial, than whom

A fairer person lost not heaven; he seemed
For dignity composed and high exploit:
But all was false and hollow; though his tongue
Dropped manna, and could make the worse appear
The better reason . . .   (II, 110—14)

Belial's counsel is for "ignoble ease and peaceful sloth"; in fact to do nothing, to accept their situation and hope that it will improve. Finally there is Mammon, whom we have already met with his eyes firmly fixed on the golden floor of Heaven. His advice is neither to strive to win back their former state nor simply to accept things as they are; but rather to seek to build on their present situation, for

. . . Our greatness will appear
The most conspicuous, when great things of small,
Useful of hurtful, prosperous of adverse
We can create, and in what place so e'er
Thrive under evil, and work ease out of pain
Through labour and endurance . . .   (II, 257—62)

Out of context these three suggestions — to hit back blindly, to accept the inevitable passively and to seek to make the most of the situation — would, I think, generally be accepted as representing steps in an ascending scale of practical and moral response to misfortune. But this is Hell, a place where the roof resembles the floor of Heaven; where in other words everything is turned upside down, morally as well as physically, so that what is good in Heaven becomes evil in Hell. Evil is the perversion of good, and for one immersed in evil as the fallen angels are immersed in Hell, to struggle against it, even though blindly, is preferable to passive acceptance, or even more to the search for ways to build on it. Events in Hell are to be judged in their context of evil, and one should not, as Belial suggests, seek to "thrive under evil".

Satan is, in a sense, the personification of evil, and whenever he enters the action the nature and working of evil are revealed. When first he moves to rebel against God he at once surrounds himself with an aura of suspicion and deceit which continues to be associated with evil throughout the poem. After God had announced his decision regarding the exaltation of the Son, a decision which was the immediate cause of the revolt, at once an element of dissembling is introduced:

So spake the omnipotent, and with his words
All seemed well pleased, all seemed, but were not all.   (V, 616—17)

Having determined on disobedience, Satan speaks first to his "next subordinate", but only in guarded terms because "more in this place / To
utter is not safe", and his first move is to deceive his own followers.
"Assemble thou / Of all those myriads we lead as chief" he orders his
subordinate, "Tell them . . . I am to haste . . .

> Homeward with flying march where we possess
> The quarters of the north, there to prepare
> Fit entertainment to receive our king,
> The great Messiah . . .
> Who speedily through all the hierarchies
> Intends to pass triumphant, and give laws.   (V, 685–93)

When Satan has his followers safely assembled in his northern strong-
hold, his deceitfulness takes a different form — that of rhetoric, of fine
words, of the "calumnious art / Of counterfeited truth" (V, 770–71) — in
a speech which one foremost critic unfortunately once chose to illustrate
his belief that Milton often paid more attention to the sound of his verse
than to its sense.[3] But his criticism should have been directed not at
Milton but at Satan, for the speech serves directly to show the emptiness
of fine words when put to the wrong ends, when they are intended to
deceive more than to illuminate — as do also some of those utterances of
Satan in Hell which have tended to win the admiration of readers.

This same pattern of emergent deceit accompanying the appearance of
evil is repeated even more forcefully with Eve as the effects of her disobedience in eating the apple work a swift transformation in her, leading
her to move rapidly from the idea of deceiving Adam by not telling him
about the apple in order to give herself the advantage over him, to reach
finally extraordinary heights of self-deception:

> . . . But to Adam in what sort
> Shall I appear? Shall I to him make known
> As yet my change, and give him to partake
> Full happiness with me, or rather not,
> But keep the odds of knowledge in my power
> Without copartner? So to add what wants
> In female sex, the more to draw his love,
> And render me more equal, and perhaps,
> A thing not undesirable, sometime
> Superior; for inferior, who is free?
> This may be well: but what if God have seen,

---

3. T. S. Eliot in his essay *Milton* published in 1936, in which he sought to show the
pernicious influence of Milton on other poets. Eliot more or less recanted this
view in a later essay, also entitled *Milton* (1947). The earlier essay and a selection
from the later are to be found in *Selected Prose of T. S. Eliot*, ed. Frank Kermode
(1975).

And death ensue? Then shall I be no more,
And Adam wedded to another Eve,
Shall live with her enjoying, I extinct;
A death to think. Confirmed then I resolve
Adam shall share with me in bliss or woe;
So dear I love him that with him all deaths
I could endure, without him live no life.   (IX, 816—33)

Nothing in the poem illustrates more dramatically the degrading effect of evil than this transformation of Eve; and it is heightened even further after Adam too has resolved to eat the apple and Eve speaks again:

Were it I thought death menaced would ensue
This my attempt, I would sustain alone
The worst and not persuade thee rather die
Deserted, than oblige thee with a fact
Pernicious to thy peace . . .   (IX, 977—81)

But more important perhaps even than the degradation is this theme of deception, of the deception of others and of the self, the wilful or unknowing confusion of what is with what seems to be, or can be made to seem to be, which is consistently associated with evil in the poem. It is a theme most explicitly stated when Satan in the guise of a "stripling Cherub" is met by the Archangel Uriel, "one of the seven / Who in God's presence . . . / Stand ready at command and are his eyes" (III, 648—50). But even the eyes of Uriel, though they act for God, are unable to recognize the "false dissembler":

For neither man nor angel can discern
Hypocrisy, the only evil that walks
Invisible, except to God alone.   (III, 682—84)

The Uriel incident serves to link the element of deceit inherent in evil with its attractiveness, something that has been the subject of one of the most persuasive of recent interpretations of *Paradise Lost*, that suggested by Stanley Fish in his *Surprised by Sin* (1967). Fish's thesis is that those critics who have followed the poet William Blake in seeing Milton as being "of the Devil's party without knowing it"[4] have been caught, as it were, in a trap set for them by Milton, a trap designed to demonstrate just how fatally easy it is to be taken in by the attractiveness of evil. We must, as Arnold Stein, in his *Answerable Style* (1953), had also earlier insisted, listen to the framing context of the words of the narrator, which sets the events of the narrative within a system of formal values by which evil is revealed for what it is. Instead, for instance, of listening simply to the fine

---

4. In his *Marriage of Heaven and Hell* in which Blake declares that it was for this reason that "Milton wrote in fetters when he wrote of Angels and God, and at liberty when of Devils and Hell".

words of Satan in the first book as he strives to rally both himself and his
followers, we must also listen to the narrator when he comments:

> ... but he his wonted pride
> Soon recollecting, with high words, that bore
> Semblance of worth, not substance, gently raised
> Their fainting courage ...   (I, 527–30)

These words adjust our response. I do not think that Fish's interpretation
provides all the answers to all the problems, all the undercurrents of the
poem, but it does highlight how the poem reveals the superficial attractiveness of evil and the ease with which one can become involved in it.

A key passage of the poem as it relates to the matter of the confusion
of what is with what seems to be is provided by Adam's account to
Raphael of the influence which Eve has on him. The passage is a relatively
long one and I shall be discussing it in a wider context in connection with
Eve's role in the narrative, but it is of sufficient importance to justify also
quoting it here. The lines are part of Adam's account to Raphael of how
Eve came to be created. He "must confess to find" he says,

> In all things else delight indeed, but such
> As used or not, works in the mind no change,
> Nor vehement desire, these delicacies
> I mean of taste, sight, smell, herbs, fruits, and flowers.
> Walks, and the melody of birds: but here,
> Far otherwise, transported I behold,
> Transported touch; here passion first I felt,
> Commotion strange, in all enjoyments else
> Superior and unmoved, here only weak
> Against the charm of beauty's powerful glance.
> ... well I understand in the prime end
> Of nature her the inferior, in the mind
> And inward faculties, which most excel;
> ... yet when I approach
> Her loveliness, so absolute she seems
> And in her self complete, so well to know
> Her own, that what she wills to do or say
> Seems wisest, virtuousest, discreetest, best;
> All higher knowledge in her presence falls
> Degraded, wisdom in discourse with her
> Looses discountenanced, and like folly shows.   (VIII, 524–53)

I shall, as I say, discuss this passage in more detail elsewhere, but immediately obvious is the extent to which in this crucial matter — its crucial
nature is emphasized by its being placed in Book VIII, almost the last
thing before the climax of the action, the onset of the fall itself — the
extent to which in this crucial matter Adam is led away by what seems to
be from what is, by the semblance rather than the substance of worth.

This matter of Adam's attitude to Eve will also serve conveniently to make an important, or at least useful distinction between sin and evil, a distinction not always maintained in the poem. Eve's beauty is not itself evil. Nor is it sinful for her to be beautiful. Sin is a matter of choice, an act of will leading the individual in one direction rather than another. Evil is what results from a wrong choice being made. Hell is a place of evil; that is, it is a place created by Satan and his followers when they choose to disobey rather than to obey God, and it is perpetuated by them as they continue in their disobedience. To return to Adam and Eve, it might be thought sinful for Eve wilfully to use her beauty to influence Adam to act wrongly, her beauty thereby becoming an external evil to Adam. Evil is thus both the source and consequence of sin; sin itself is the act of will deriving from evil and resulting in further evil. This point is made by Adam in a passage mentioned earlier, when in commenting on her dream he tells Eve that "Evil into the mind of god or man / May come and go, so unapproved, and leave / No spot or blame behind" (V, 117–19). It is only when evil is "approved", when it results in an act of will, that questions of sin arise. And when Milton in *Areopagitica* declares that "this is the doom which Adam fell into of knowing good and evil, that is to say, of knowing good by evil", he is saying that we know what is right or good to choose by knowing the *consequences* of making the wrong choice. That is, evil, but not necessarily sin, has as a result of the fall become the means of our knowing good; we do not actually have to *do* wrong in order to recognize what is wrong.

This distinction between sin and evil, which is perhaps blurred by there being no comparable word to stand against sin, as good stands against evil, is clear enough; and indeed it may be central to the problem with which this essay began — the existence of evil in a world created wholly by God. Indeed it may be necessary to rephrase the question in order to ask not about the existence of evil but the emergence of sin. It is stressed, for instance, that Eve right up to the very moment of the fall is "yet sinless"; and the allegorical figure of Sin, whom Satan meets at the gates of Hell and who claims to be both his daughter and the mother of his offspring Death, speaks of a time

> In heaven, when at the assembly, and in sight
> Of all the seraphim with thee combined
> In bold conspiracy against heaven's king,
> . . . a goddess armed,
> Out of thy head I sprung.   (II, 749–58)

The emergence of sin, then, is dependent on the actual mental act. On the occasion of Eve's dream prompted by Satan again, Adam says:

> This uncouth dream, of evil sprung I fear;
> Yet evil whence? In thee can harbour none,
> Created pure . . .   (V, 98–100)

It may be that here Adam is missing the point. It is less perhaps that Eve is "pure" in the sense of free of evil that he should be worrying about, than that she should be free of the potentiality for sin, for wilfully approving or acting on evil when it is presented to her. And of this potentiality we have had some suggestion already in the poem — in, for instance, the account she gives of her reaction to her own creation — while it has already been argued that without such potentiality she would not be, as God claims, free — that is, free to sin, free to fall.

There seems to be no escape from the conclusion that in so far as he is presented to us in *Paradise Lost*, man was created with a will, if not actually "tainted", then at least as much disposed towards making the wrong choice as the right one, as much disposed towards sin as to its opposite. This much seems indisputable, even from the evidence of God's words alone. But if the wrong choice, that is sin, is the result of evil, we still have to ask Adam's question "Yet evil whence?". This is one point where the poem, through some words of God quoted earlier, purports to make a clear distinction between angels and men, or at least between fallen angels and fallen men. "The first sort" God tells the Son, referring to Satan and his followers,

> . . . by their own suggestion fell
> Self-tempted self-depraved; man falls deceived
> By the other first . . .   (III, 129–31)

There are immediate objections to this. Firstly, Satan's followers were as much tempted by their leader's rhetoric as was Eve, and their fall was no more the result of their own suggestion; and, secondly, while Eve may have been deceived by the "other", Adam's decision to follow her in eating the apple was a clear act of will in which if there was any deception it would seem to have been purely self-deception. But even beyond this superficial and obviously untenable level it is still equally clear that no real distinction can be made. Satan, Adam and Eve all made their wrong choices, all sinned, immediately as a direct result of forces within themselves — self-pride, ambition, desire for knowledge or power, love, uxoriousness, physical passion, call it what you will — forces within themselves responding to external pressures: in Satan's case the elevation of the Son, in Eve's the temptation offered her by Satan, in Adam's the attraction of Eve. These external pressures were different at least in that for Satan the call was towards obedience while for Adam and Eve it was towards disobedience. But this seems largely irrelevant; the evil from which their sin immediately derived lay within themselves.

The Christian tradition had, of course, seen the fall as an act directly inspired by Satan. But this is not the case with *Paradise Lost*, which seems far more concerned to give a psychological validity and complexity to the simple facts of the Genesis story. And, psychologically, if sin is an act of will, then the cause of that act must also lie within the individual. An act of will is not the direct result of an external stimulus like a knee jerk. The external stimulus must have something on which to act in order to produce the resultant act of will. Adam, in the same speech arising from Eve's dream, gives us an outline of Renaissance psychology on this point:

> . . . But know that in the soul
> Are many lesser faculties, that serve
> Reason as chief. Among these fancy next
> Her office holds; of all external things,
> Which the five watchful senses represent,
> She forms imaginations, airy shapes,
> Which reason, joining or disjoining, frames
> All what we affirm or what deny, and call
> Our knowledge or opinion; then retires
> Into her private cell when nature rests.
> Oft in her absence mimic fancy wakes
> To imitate her; but misjoining shapes,
> Wild work produces oft, and most in dreams,
> Ill matching words and deeds long past or late.
> Some such resemblances methinks, I find
> Of our last evening's talk in this thy dream,
> But with addition strange . . .   (V, 100–116)

The suggestion here, and it is one that is reinforced throughout the poem as well as being completely in accord with popular seventeenth-century thought, is that sin is likely to arise when external stimuli (here what Adam calls the "addition strange" but we know as Satan's influence exercised while Eve is asleep) act on the "lesser faculties", particularly fancy or imagination, so that they no longer "serve reason as chief". Man being a rational creature will behave rationally, that is rightly, so long as his reason remains in control. Only when the reason is displaced from its position of control is he in danger; a point of fundamental importance in relation to the role Milton gives to Eve, whom we have already seen as able to influence Adam into confusing what is with what seems to be, as one of whom he says "all higher knowledge in her presence falls / Degraded".

We have been concerned thus far mainly with evil and sin as they relate to man as he was created — that is, in his unfallen state — when as we have seen evil was in a sense a necessity in order that man might be in a position to exercise the freedom given him by God to sin or not as he chose. After the fall, it would seem that evil remains necessary to man, but for a different reason. Because he is no longer free in the original sense, he no longer needs evil in order to allow the opportunity for free choice; but he does need it in order to be able to recognize good. As part of a general account of hierarchy, Raphael makes a distinction for Adam between "discursive" and "intuitive" reasoning. Of these, he says, "discourse / Is oftest yours, the latter most is ours, / Differing but in degree, of kind the same" (V, 488–90). That is, the angels reason primarily intuitively, man primarily discursively. The difference is in degree only, however, both kinds of reason being open to some extent to both men and angels, and the poem implies that one thing which unfallen man knew intuitively was good, and further that this was something lost at the fall. These are facts that cannot be readily illustrated as regards man, but in the parallel case of the fallen angels they can. When Satan is challenged by the Seraph Abdiel for urging rebellion against his creator, Satan replies by demanding empirical evidence:

> That we were formed then, say'st thou? And the work
> Of secondary hands, by task transferred
> From Father to his Son? Strange point and new!
> Doctrine which we would know whence learned: who saw
> When this creation was? Remember'st thou
> Thy making, while the maker gave thee being?
> We know no time when we were not as now;
> Know none before us, self-begot, self-raised
> By our own quickening power . . .   (V, 853–61)

Here Satan, already fallen, has lost or chooses to ignore the evidence of his intuitive understanding, and requires instead the kind of evidence that can be argued discursively. The same we may assume is true of man after the fall, and Milton in fact confirms this is in a passage we have already referred to from *Areopagitica,* in which he suggests that the "doom" Adam fell into at the fall was of "knowing good and evil, that is of knowing good by evil". Thus from being a necessity for the freedom of man's will, evil becomes instead a necessary means of knowing good.

In the account of the fallen world given by Michael to Adam in the final two books of the poem the emphasis is on external evil, on the evil which results and multiplies from the sin of the fall. Pitted against this evil, however, is the strength of the few just men — Noah, Abraham, Ezekiel and the other so-called types of Christ — whose inner strength stands against the power of evil. And the poem ends with a return to an emphasis on the inner, essentially spiritual nature both of evil and of the defence against it. As the Archangel Michael comes towards the end of his prophetic narrative, he tells Adam of the coming of the Messiah and of his promised defeat of Satan. Adam is overcome with joy, and demands to hear "where and when / They fight, what stroke shall bruise the Victor's heel". But Michael admonishes him:

> . . . Dream not of their fight
> As of a duel, or the local wounds
> Of head or heel: not therefore joins the Son

Manhood to Godhead, with more strength to foil
Thy enemy; nor so is overcome
Satan . . .   (XII, 386—91)

The victory of good over evil will not be by means of physical battle.
Rather "he wo comes thy saviour shall recure", he says,

Not by destroying Satan, but his works
In thee and in thy seed. Nor can this be,
But by fulfilling that which thou didst want,
Obedience to the law of God . . .
The law of God exact he shall fulfil
Both by obedience and by love, though love
Alone fulfil the Law . . .   (XII, 394—404)

And later in response to Adam's coming to understand that "suffering for
Truth's sake / Is fortitude to highest victory", Michael tells him:

This having learned, thou hast attained the sum
Of wisdom . . .
. . . only add
Deeds to thy knowledge answerable, add faith,
Add virtue, patience, temperance . . .
. . . then wilt thou not be loath
To leave this Paradise, but shalt possess
A paradise within thee, happier far.   (XII, 575—87)

Just as man's first battle with evil had been lost within the mind, so it is
within the mind of man that the battle will finally be won. Except that
here, instead of the emphasis being on the spreading out of the effects
of the fall into the world beyond the mind, on the destruction of the
outer paradise of the Garden, the emphasis is now wholly on the achieve-
ment of an inner paradise. The fruits of the victory, as well as the battle
itself, will be essentially within the mind.

4

I Created Him Free

If "evil" is at the heart of *Paradise Lost*, then "freedom" is closely associated with it, and any consideration of the nature of freedom as it is revealed in the poem will inevitably take us over some of the same ground as that covered in the exploration of evil. And just as the origin and workings of evil were found to be less than straightforward, so the concept of freedom is complex and elusive. One result of man's "first disobedience" we learn in the poem's opening lines to be the "loss of Eden", and with it the loss of the perfect freedom that characterized life in the Garden. But at the very end of the poem, as Adam and Eve are being expelled from Paradise, we are told that "the world was all before them"; and it is difficult for the reader not at least to share the "doubt" of Adam as he listens to Michael's prophetic narrative of what is to be the outcome of man's fall. The freedom that faces Adam and Eve as they leave the Garden may be infinitely more dangerous and exacting than the one they are losing, but many will feel that its possibilities are equally greater. The word "free", together with the associated "freed", "freedom", "freely" and "free will", occurs sixty-nine times in *Paradise Lost*. Concepts of freedom, in fact, pervade the poem and like those of evil are at the very centre of the paradoxical image of the human condition that it presents. What is it to be free?

The freedom with which man was created is presented to us in *Paradise Lost* ostensibly as meaning two things, both of which are likely to present difficulties to the modern reader: firstly free will, residing in the opportunity for choice, specifically the opportunity for choice between the absolute alternatives of good and evil; and secondly the freedom that comes with absolute belief (in this case absolute belief in God) and that is lost when the belief is lost.[1] The problems begin to arise when these two

---

1. The sense in which I use the term "absolute belief" and the freedom that comes with it may need some explanation. If I may use an analogy, if one believes absolutely that capital punishment is wrong, then one is freed from any real concern with the rights and wrongs of any particular instance of it. It is wrong and that is all there is to it. On the other hand, of course, one may feel restricted in not being allowed to use one's own judgement. But once the absolute belief is lost, then each case must be considered on its merits and any judgement on it will be hedged around by the thousand and one circumstances which need to be taken account of and which may be felt to cloud the central issue. In this sense one may feel that one's judgement has become the prisoner of circumstances, unable to

concepts are taken together, when it is apparent that the first kind of freedom can only be exercised at the risk of the second, which in turn may
well prove to be the more important. A man standing on the edge of a high
cliff may be perfectly free either to step back or to jump over. Except that
by making the first choice he both retains his future freedom in relation
to that particular decision and also continues to experience the freedom
that comes from feeling firm ground under his feet; at least this is something that he is free from worrying about. But if he jumps he no longer
has the first kind of freedom and his future freedom of action in other
respects is at best questionable. Certainly he is free to jump or not, but is
freedom with such dire consequences for making the wrong choice really
freedom at all? The analogy may not be exact, but the reader may find
it plausible, and not altogether be convinced by the reality of such freedom — be tempted perhaps to think of jumping anyway on the chance of
finding a less restricted and restricting form of freedom.

That freedom has these two basic aspects is implied by God in his
statement to the Son regarding man's situation:

> I formed them free, and free they must remain,
> Till they enthrall themselves: I else must change
> Their nature . . .   (III, 124–26)

That is, as I have said, man is created free to choose between good and
evil, and also with the freedom that results from absolute belief in the
goodness of God, until by his own free choice he loses both kinds of freedom. And this dichotomy of freedom and "self-enthralment" is enlarged
upon by Abdiel before the war in Heaven, in reply to Satan's taunt that

> At first I thought that liberty and heaven
> To heavenly souls had been all one; but now
> I see that most through sloth had rather serve.   (VI, 164–66)

To which Abdiel responds, stressing first the freedom deriving from true
belief:

> Unjustly thou deprav'st it with the name
> Of servitude to serve whom God ordains,
> Or nature . . .
> . . . This is servitude,
> To serve the unwise, or him who hath rebelled
> Against his worthier, as thine now serve thee,
> Thy self not free, but to thy self enthralled.   (VI, 174–81)

Freedom in the sense that is here upheld by Abdiel has as its concomitants love and obedience. This is stated most clearly by Raphael to Adam,

move freely in any direction. Or, to take a different kind of example, the soldier
who simply has to do as he is told, every decision being made for him, may in a
sense feel freer than when he returns to civilian life and must make his own
decisions.

though it is reiterated or implied on a variety of occasions throughout the poem:

> My self and all the angelic host that stand
> In sight of God enthroned, our happy state
> Hold, as you yours, while our obedience holds;
> On other surety none; freely we serve,
> Because we freely love, as in our will
> To love or not ...   (V, 535—40)

These three things, freedom, love and obedience, cannot be separated, but truly exist only in relation to each other. There is no freedom except that accompanying absolute obedience rendered for love; no real love except that manifested in obedience freely given; no true obedience except that freely granted from love. It is the lack of these concomitants of freedom, for example, that causes Christ in *Paradise Regained* to reject Satan's offer of help in freeing the lost tribes of Israel:

> As for those captive tribes, themselves were they
> Who wrought their own captivity, fell off
> From God to worship calves ...
> Should I of these the liberty regard,
> Who freed, as to their ancient patrimony,
> Unhumbled, unrepentent, unreformed
> Headlong would follow ...
> ... No, let them serve
> Their enemies, who serve idols with God.   (*P.R.*, III, 414—32)

The tribes have neither the love nor the obedience towards God which would allow them to retain their freedom if it were to be gained for them.

The self-enthralment, which man brings on himself by exercising his freedom to disobey God and with which we have seen Abdiel taunt Satan, begins to make itself apparent immediately on Satan's choice of disobedience. He at once surrounds himself with an aura of distrust and deceit. He begins to speak to his "next subordinate", but soon breaks off with "more in this place / To utter is not safe" (V, 682—83). And it is most directly expressed in the great "Satanic" soliloquy which precedes Satan's first entry into the Garden. This soliloquy makes clear that what had appeared as an arbitrary sentence passed by God on Satan and his followers — that man "shall find grace, / The other none" (III, 131—32) — is after all not this. The impossibility of grace derives not from God's withholding it, but from Satan's being unable, through his own self-enthralment, to receive it. "O, then, at last relent!" Satan demands of himself:

> ... is there no place
> Left for repentence, none for pardon left?
> None left but by submission; and that word

> Disdain forbids me, and my dread of shame
> Among the spirits beneath . . .
> This knows my punisher; therefore as far
> From granting he, as I from begging peace.   (IV, 79–104)

Like many a political figure after him, Satan has become the prisoner of his ambitions, of his need for glory and for the adulation of his followers. The freedom he sought through his rebellion has proved illusory.

The obedience on which the freedom given to man by God depends, and without which the only alternative is seen as self-enthralment, is both arbitrary and absolute. It is obedience given for its own sake, or rather obedience given simply because man wishes to give it. This means that any test, or proof, of obedience must be adherence to an arbitrary command, one for which there is no other apparent reason to obey it than obedience itself. From Raphael we learn that this applies equally to the angels. He has to ask Adam for information about his, Adam's, creation, because he himself

> . . . that day was absent, as befell,
> Bound on a voyage uncouth and obscure,
> Far on excursion towards the gates of hell,
>
> .   .   .   .   .
> Not that they durst without his leave attempt;
> But us he sends upon his high behests
> For state, as sovereign king, and to inure
> Our prompt obedience. . .   (VIII, 229–40)

Similarly the prohibition placed for Adam and Eve on eating the fruit of the tree of the knowledge of good and evil is arbitrary, something which is suggested in the very first lines of the poem if they are read carefully:

> Of man's first disobedience, and the fruit . . .

If we pause here, giving as we should the line division its due, the fruit is momentarily related back to the disobedience; until we move on:

> Of that forbidden tree. . .   (I, 2)

when the grammatical structure takes over, and the fruit becomes that of the tree rather than the disobedience. But this is a poem, in which poetical structure should take precedence over prose, as it is ultimately seen to do here. "Death . . . and all our woe" *are* the fruit of man's disobedience, not some property of the apple. Adam and Eve know the tree to be "the only sign of our obedience" (IV, 428); they know that they must not eat the fruit, but know of no other reason than obedience why they should not do so. This is essential, because if there were any other reason — if the fruit itself were poisonous, for instance — then they might refrain from it for that reason rather than from obedience. It is, indeed, part of the error into which Eve is led by Satan that she sees the tree itself as conferring special powers which God, for reasons of His own, wishes to deprive them of. Eating the apple does indeed give new knowledge, that of good and evil. "Since our eyes / Opened we find indeed" says Adam after the fall,

> . . . and find we know
> Both good and evil, good lost, and evil got.   (IX, 1071–72)

But it is the disobedience involved in eating the apple, not the apple itself, that is the source of this new knowledge.

This then appears to be the freedom with which man is endowed by God on his creation — freedom dependent on absolute, arbitrary obedience freely and unquestioningly given. It is a concept of freedom not unknown in the twentieth century, freedom which is deemed to result from the same absolute obedience to some leader, or perhaps to an idea or belief, obedience which is given freely and without question because of the complete, unwavering regard in which the leader or idea is held. The result is a life in which no demand is made on man except his willingly given obedience, since in return for that obedience he has no need to worry about the thousand and one "accidents" of life which might otherwise have to be taken into account in reaching any decision. There is, I think, no doubt that if this is indeed the concept of true freedom presented by the poem there will be many readers who will question the reality of such freedom; will question whether the "free will" with which God insists man was created is really free in any meaningful sense, whether man is truly free in Paradise. But the more immediate question is not whether the present-day reader will ask these questions, but whether the poem itself asks them; and, if so, the answers it gives.

An important qualification of the concept of man's original freedom as we have seen it thus far may perhaps be derived from an outwardly curious statement made by Raphael to Adam. "God", he says, "made thee perfect, not immutable" (V, 524). Many readers are likely to find this statement contradictory. That which is perfect is, by virtue of its perfection, necessarily immutable. It cannot change for the better because it is already perfect, and for it to be able to change for the worse indicates that it is somehow imperfect. This reaction to the statement would I think have been even stronger in Milton's own time, when modern ideas of progress had not really taken charge, and any change was likely to be seen as being for the worse, part of the process of decay from a past golden age. What the Renaissance tended to strive for was a static, immutable perfection. Three possibilities then arise: Raphael's understanding of God's ways was showing itself to be fallible; he (or Milton) was being careless in his use of words; or some meaning other than the normal one was being given either to "perfection" or to "mutability".

As to the first possibility, God at no times describes man as perfect. The already quoted "Sufficient to have stood, though free to fall" is his dictum; and this nicely balanced arrangement seems to fit the circumstances of the narrative more accurately than does Raphael's statement. On the one occasion when God does mention man's mutability he describes his will as "though free / Yet mutable" (V, 236–37), and it could be argued that he is including the mutability within the freedom, in the sense of allowing men to change and yet to remain free. But it should be remembered that these words come within the warning which God is instructing Raphael to convey to Adam. "Whence warn him" are his very next words, "to beware / He swerve not", and in the statement itself freedom and mutability are hedged around and separated by the qualifying "though" and "yet". Raphael's words, too, that we began by considering, are within the context of the same warning. Perhaps the full passage should be quoted:

> . . . that thou art happy, owe to God;
> That thou continuest such, owe to thyself,
> That is, to thy obedience; therein stand.
> This was that caution given thee; be advised.
> God made thee perfect, not immutable;
> And good he made thee, but to persevere
> He left it in thy power . . .   (V, 520–26)

It is very difficult in the face of this not to decide that Raphael is using the word "perfect" rather loosely, and that mutability is a danger to unfallen man's happiness, the only defence against which is unchanging obedience.

Some critics, however, have argued strongly against such a static view of pre-fallen life by seeking to follow the third possibility suggested above: that of giving a special meaning to the relationship of mutability and perfection — special, that is, for the Renaissance — by which mutability becomes a change towards an even higher perfection rather than a decay away from it. Within the framework of continued obedience, they say, there is ample scope for opportunities to experience and to learn. Such an episode, for example, as Eve's first turning towards her own reflection rather than towards Adam is seen not as a sign of weakness or potential weakness but as rather the opposite; as a learning situation in which a choice is presented and the right one eventually made. Barbara Lewalski, in her "Innocence and Experience in Milton's Eden" has explored unfallen man's ability to change for the better. She asserts that life in the Garden is "radical growth and progress, a mode of life steadily increasing in complexity and challenge and difficulty but at the same time and by that very fact in perfection".[2] The tragedy of the fall for her is that it is the event which ruined our chances of developing "the rich resources and large potentialities of the human spirit". And certainly Raphael suggests a time

2. Barbara Lewalski, "Innocence and Experience in Milton's Eden", in *New Essays on Paradise Lost,* ed. Thomas Kranidas (1969), p. 88.

that "may come when men / With angels may participate" (V, 493–94), implying at least the chance of upward progress. But the limitations placed on man's aspirations are none the less clear. "Solicit not thy thoughts with matters hid" Raphael tells Adam,

> Leave them to God above, him serve and fear;
> Of other creatures, as him pleases best,
> Wherever placed, let him dispose: joy thou
> In what he gives thee, this Paradise
> And thy fair Eve; heaven is for thee too high
> To know what passes there; be lowly wise:
> Think only what concerns thee and thy being;
> Dream not of other worlds, what creatures there
> Live . . .   (VIII, 168–76)

I am reminded of a veteran T.V. actor who having tried to be helpful in a slight mishap during filming of a show and been rebuked by the director, made the rueful aside to the audience: "Remember your lines and leave the furniture alone". Adam's reward is to be won only "If ye be found obedient, and retain / Unalterably firm his love entire" (V, 501–2); and we should remember, too, that the ultimate purpose of freedom is that thereby man may render true obedience to God. "Not free" asks God,

> . . . what proof could they have given sincere
> Of true allegiance, constant faith, or love,
> Where only what they needs must do, appeared,
> Not what they would? What praise could they receive,
> What pleasure I from such obedience paid,
> When will and reason . . .
> Made passive both, had served necessity,
> Not me? . . .   (III, 103–11)

The problem is highlighted in a scene between Adam and Eve which occurs significantly immediately prior to the fall and in a sense is the immediate occasion of it. The scene begins with a suggestion from Eve to Adam that as the Garden is "tending to wild" they should divide their labours in order to get more done. Adam at first praises her:

> . . . for nothing lovelier can be found
> In woman, than to study household good,
> And good works in her husband to promote.   (IX, 232–34)

"But", he says, "other doubt possesses me, lest harm / Befall thee, severed from me" (IX, 251–52). The matter now becomes, for Eve, a test of her worth and independence:

> But that thou shouldst my firmness therefore doubt
> To God or thee, because we have a foe
> May tempt it, I expected not to hear.
> .   .   .   .   .

His fraud is then thy fear, which plain infers
Thy equal fear that my firm faith and love
Can by this fraud be shaken or seduced.   (IX, 279–87)

Adam replies that it is not his "diffidence" of her strength that concerns
him, but rather that temptation, even if unsuccessful "at least asperses /
The tempted with dishonour foul" (IX, 296–97). But Eve, who still
thinks "less attributed to her faith sincere", turns the argument to the
question of freedom. "How are we to be happy, still in fear of harm?"
she asks,

And what is faith, love, virtue, unassayed
Alone, without exterior help sustained?   (IX, 335–36)

Here Eve, by claiming that faith, love, virtue are not real if they can only
be sustained with external help, uses the very argument against Adam that
Milton had used in his *Areopagitica* when in a famous passage he had
declared that "I cannot praise a fugitive and cloistered virtue, unexercised
and unbreathed, that never sallies out and sees her adversary, but slinks
out of the race where that immortal garland is to be run for, not without
dust and heat"; and Adam is left in the position of being, like God in
relation to Satan's threat to himself, unable to protect Eve further without
interfering with her freedom:

Go; for thy stay, not free, absents thee more;
Go in thy native innocence, rely
On what thou hast of virtue, summon all,
For God towards thee hath done his part, do thine.   (IX, 372–75)

Eve is wrong. Adam for her is in God's place and ought to be obeyed. The
fact that she insists on her independence leads directly to her temptation
and fall. But it is still difficult for the reader not to feel the force of Eve's
argument; and if only for its echo of *Areopagitica* not to believe that
Milton would also have felt it, have felt that despite the arguments to the
contrary, despite the attractiveness of life in the Garden and its promise of
even greater bliss to come, the kind of freedom it offered was too limited.

In giving way to Eve in this scene Adam recognizes that man's future
happiness and security is in his own keeping:

. . . within himself
The danger lies, yet lies within his power:
Against his will he can receive no harm.   (IX, 348–50)

And on the point of the fall being purely the result of man's misuse of his
freedom, Milton's God is bluntly assertive. He created man "sufficient to
have stood" and He becomes almost obsessive about reiterating the fact
of man's responsibility at every point. He anticipates the charge that His
foreknowledge denies the fact of man's free will and does His best to
refute it:

> . . . if I foreknew,
> Foreknowledge had no influence on their fault,
> Which had no less proved certain unforeknown.   (III, 117–19)

And His emissary Raphael echoes God in his forceful testimony to Adam:

> And good he made thee, but to persevere
> He left it in thy power, ordained thy will
> By nature free, not over-ruled by fate
> Inextricable, or strict necessity.   (V, 525–28)

Even after the fall, though Adam may blame God for having created Eve, or even for that matter himself, neither he nor Eve blames God for their act, only each other. And the narrator, speaking for God, hammers home the nails of blame:

> For still they knew, and ought to have still remembered,
> The high injunction not to taste the fruit,
> Whoever tempted; which they not obeying
> Incurred, what could they less, the penalty,
> And manifold in sin, deserved to fall.   (X, 12–16)

But the tone and dramatic structure of *Paradise Lost* combine to undermine such a straightforward position. God knows that man will fall and as we have seen puts the blame fairly and squarely on the way that he chooses to exercise his free will. But for the reader, and this will be explored more fully in other essays, the circumstances leading up to and surrounding the fall persuade him rather of its inevitability, persuade him that man will fall not because he wills it but because he is what he is. There is a constant suggestion that man is "frail" — "innocent frail man", as he is described by the narrator as Satan approaches him for the first time (IV, 11). And alongside this is the constant suggestion of the seductive power of evil — potent, resilient, anything but frail. We are never allowed to forget that in this contest with evil man must rely on himself alone, that God cannot interfere lest He diminish man's freedom; or that though "perfect" he is "mutable". Nor is it to be forgotten that though evil is essentially repellently ugly, Satan's pose as a "stripling Cherub" is so convincing that it can deceive the Archangel Uriel, one of those who serve as the eyes of God. Man is optimistic that he can resist evil. Adam overestimates the strength of himself and of Eve. He is incredulous in the face of Raphael's hints that they might disobey God:

> What meant that caution joined, *if ye be found
> Obedient*? Can we want obedience then
> To him, or possibly his love desert
> Who formed us from the dust . . .   (V, 513–16)

And Eve underestimates the strength of evil in Satan, mistaking his pride for honour. She does not "much expect / A foe so proud will first the weaker seek" (IX, 382–83). Such naive confidence in Adam and Eve makes them seem pathetically frail, and evil in Satan almost invincible.

Man's resistance to evil is tested on more than one occasion, and the tendencies of personality that are to prove fatal to Adam and Eve are exposed and expanded: Eve's leaning towards vanity, towards self-love, Adam's tendency towards inordinate curiosity, and towards placing Eve above himself and even above God. And with each illustration man seems to grow frailer, the temptation to evil stronger, the reader more anticipant and the fall more imminent. The reader may, like the fallen angels in Hell reason high "Of providence, foreknowledge, will and fate, / Fixed fate, free will, foreknowledge absolute" and be, like them, in "wandering mazes lost" (II, 559–61). But, though he may hope that Adam and Eve will not fall, he knows that they will – and not altogether because their destiny is a commonplace of Christian history. The knowledge, the inevitability, seems to grow out of the poem itself, and to deny the assertion of their freedom. The freedom given them by God seems impossible to retain, though theoretically they have the stamina to retain it. The state of the Garden itself images the state of their freedom. As the fall approaches they find it increasingly difficult to maintain; and an element of irony enters when Eve uses the excuse of the disordered garden to leave Adam's side and fall into the trap set for her by Satan. Adam and Eve are "sufficient to have stood"; but "sufficient" suggests an almost calculated precision, and in human affairs may more often than not prove "insufficient". It is not so much God's foreknowledge, but the reader's foreknowledge gained from the imaginative thrust of the poem, which contradicts the assertion of man's absolute freedom of will before the fall.

This apparent contradiction has been the subject of various interpretations. At one extreme there is the view that it signifies a self-deception in Milton, a proof that in spite of what Milton appeared to believe he really believed that man was not created free in "both will and deed" (V, 549), but was fated to fall, not supported by God but betrayed by Him; that man's will is by no means "to her own inclining left / In even scale" (X, 46–47). At the opposite extreme is the view that the contradiction is indeed only apparent and represents a deception of others by Milton; that while the discriminating reader will recognize the truth, the more prone to error will be trapped, as it were, into falling alongside Adam and Eve, and be thereby brought to realize more clearly the nature and dangers of evil. The first kind of approach accepts the contradiction as a means of condemning God in order to exonerate man; the second denies that there is any contradiction in order to "justify" God and condemn man, two views perhaps best represented by, respectively, William Empson's *Milton's God* and Stanley Fish's *Surprised by Sin.*

But is it necessary to accept either of these approaches to the exclusion of the other? In the twentieth century it is no longer possible for any but a small minority of readers to accept, at least in any simple straightforward way, *Paradise Lost* as a justification of "the ways of God to man". To insist on interpreting it as such is for most readers to make of the poem what it has been called, a monument to dead ideas; and despite Milton's stated intention it may be more profitable at first to approach *Paradise Lost* as a great exploration, rather than as a great argument; to accept for the time being its apparent contradictions as arising from psychological exploration rather than moral argument. The image of the human condition revealed by the exploration may serve to accentuate the pressure on man to exercise his free will against God in response to the demands of his humanity, and as a consequence also to accentuate the tenuousness of freedom based on absolute belief and obedience. But this does not mean that the freedoms with which man was created are to be dismissed as meaningless, or that the whole Garden episode is to be seen as irrelevant to man's development. On the contrary, we can still respond to the beauty and harmony of the Garden, still accept Barbara Lewalski's view of the potential richness for the human spirit of life in it. Indeed if the poem is to yield its full meaning then we must do so. If the Garden, and the kind of freedom it stands for, though destined inevitably to be lost, is not felt to be somehow worth keeping, if its loss is not a source of pity and of a sense of waste, then it will not be a fitting balance to the freedom of the "paradise within" of which Milton felt man to be capable and the possibility of which could bring us back finally to the ultimate justification of God's ways.

Before the fall the freedom enjoyed by man was his by nature: "free they must remain /" says God, "I else must change / Their nature" (III, 124–26). This freedom was lost at the fall, as is made clear to Adam by Michael:

> . . . yet know withal,
> Since thy original lapse, true liberty
> Is lost . . .   (XII, 82–84)

After the fall the position is less straightforward. We know that by God's promise man will be saved:

> Man shall not quite be lost, but saved who will,
> Yet not of will in him, but grace in me
> Freely vouchsafed; once more I will renew
> His lapsed powers, though forfeit and enthralled
> By sin to foul exorbitant desires:
> Upheld by me, yet once more he shall stand
> On even ground against his mortal foe.   (III, 173–79)

The Christian position, as it had been put by Saint Augustine, for instance, was that, man's will having been tainted by the fall, the grace of God was required to renew it. This is not quite what the poem says, either in this passage or in its total imaginative effect. Let him be "saved who will / But not of will in him but grace in me". Milton seems to want to have it both ways: to put the emphasis on the need for man to will his own salvation, his own escape from the "self-enthralment" of the fall, while at the same time paying at least lip service to the doctrine of grace.

And this seems to be the case with Adam and Eve in the scene which signals their first move toward redemption. Prompted by Eve's wish to take on herself the blame for the fall, Adam turns from his own bitter thoughts to a much less self-obsessed, more humble attitude, and they find themselves again able to speak to God:

> Thus they in lowliest plight repentent stood
> Praying, for from the mercy-seat above
> Prevenient grace descending had removed
> The stony from their hearts . . .   (XI, 1–4)

Here again the problem is the same. These lines suggest that it is "pre-venient grace" that has removed "the stony from their hearts". But reading the preceding episode we must feel that it is Adam and Eve themselves, particularly Eve, who have done this as a conscious act of will. If we feel anything in this scene it is Eve's pitting herself against Adam's bitterness and winning him to her new found humility; and the subsequent introduction of grace seems almost an afterthought introduced to preserve orthodoxy, as it seems also to have been in the passage I quoted earlier. Freedom, which in the unfallen world was given to man by God and had only to be preserved by "long obedience", in the fallen world seems for Milton something to be hard won by the exercise of the will against difficult odds. Odds which in the case of Satan, for instance, are beyond him, for as we have seen it is not God's refusal to grant him grace which stands in the way of his repentence but his own inability to will that redemption for himself. At the opposite extreme, in *Paradise Regained,* we see Christ, as man, pit his will successfully against the power of evil.

What we have just seen concerning the relationship after the fall between grace and the renewal of man's freedom is only another aspect of the whole inward movement of the poem, of the way in which final answers are to be found within the mind of man. From this same point of view, we might look back finally at the concept of freedom and of how freedom is lost. Hitherto we have treated freedom as something deriving from unfallen man's loving obedience given to God, freedom which is lost when that obedience is compromised. A rather different though not necessarily incompatible view of freedom is suggested by Adam just before the fall, when he is endeavouring to persuade Eve to remain with him, and not to go off to garden on her own:

> Against his will he can receive no harm.
> But God left free the will, for what obeys

> Reason is free, and reason he made right,
> But bid her well beware, and still erect,
> Lest by some fair appearing good surprised,
> She dictate false, and misinform the will
> To do what God expressly hath forbid.   (IX, 350–56)

Here it would seem that adherence to "reason" is what constitutes freedom; and that disobedience is an outcome of the loss of this freedom rather than the cause of it. Action that is in accordance with reason is free; and it is when reason, and the freedom of action that results when reason is in control, are lost that disobedience follows. So long as man acts at the behest of reason he will act in his own best interests, in the interests of his freedom which, of course, includes obedience to God. The same point with regard to the loss of freedom is made by Michael, in defence of the existence of tyranny. "True liberty", he says " . . . always with right reason dwells":

> Reason in man obscured, or not obeyed,
> Immediately inordinate desires
> And upstart passions catch the government
> From reason, and to servitude reduce
> Man till then free. Therefore since he permits
> Within himself unworthy powers to reign
> Over free reason, God in judgement just,
> Subjects him from without to violent lords;
> Who oft as undeservedly enthral
> His outward freedom . . .   (XII, 86–95)

Just as with his redemption and the "inner freedom" that would ultimately derive from it, it would seem that man's loss of freedom — not simply the cause of that loss but the loss itself — is something which lies within his own psyche, and the role of God is at least one degree removed. Freedom is obedience not so much directly to God as to the dictates of reason; which may, of course, be claimed to be the same thing, though it sounds rather more like the God of the philosophers rather than that of the theologians. This however leads us to a consideration of the role of Eve, as the immediate apparent cause of Adam's loss of his original freedom; which is the subject of the essay to follow.

5
Eve

Perhaps the simplest, most beautiful, and most significant of all the images in *Paradise Lost* is that of joined hands, the symbol of the marriage bond. When we first meet Adam and Eve in the Garden they are hand in hand:

> So hand in hand they passed, the loveliest pair
> That ever since in love's embraces met.　　(IV, 321–22)

And as they pass from our sight at the end of the poem on their way to exile in the unknown world beyond they are again hand in hand:

> They hand in hand with wandering steps and slow,
> Through Eden took their solitary way.　　(XII, 648–49)

But between these two scenes there is the fall, and here the symbol that introduces it is not the joining but the parting of hands. As Eve turns to leave Adam, thereby exposing herself to Satan's attack,

> . . . from her husband's hand her hand
> Soft she withdrew . . .　　(IX, 385–86)

Here even the formal structure of the verse reinforces the image: the line division for the moment identifies "her hand" by apposition with "her husband's hand", but only for the moment until the bond is broken by the intrusion of the new line. Fallen or unfallen, the destiny of Adam and Eve depends on the bond between them. It is not for nothing that their wedding bower is placed at the very centre of the universe of the poem, at the "still centre of the turning world"; or that Satan sees them as "Imparadised in one another's arms" (IV, 506). For Adam and Eve, their true paradise is ultimately not that of the Garden; that may be seen as no more than an outward symbol of the perfect harmony that exists between them, a harmony that even Satan recognizes as their real paradise. This essay will explore the nature of this relationship between Adam and Eve, and in particular the role which it gives to Eve in the events of the poem, a role which makes her one of the most fascinating women of literature.

The formal aspect of their relationship is established by the narrator on their first appearance before us. They are formed

> He for God only, she for God in him　　(IV, 299)

and this entirely dependent position – one, incidentally, which would

have been universally and unquestioningly accepted in Milton's own time
— is acknowledged by Eve on numerous occasions, as for instance when
she speaks in our hearing for the first time:

> . . . O thou for whom
> And from whom I was formed flesh of thy flesh,
> And without whom am to no end, my guide
> And head . . .   (IV, 440–43)

This dutifully correct kind of beginning to her sometimes not so correct
utterances, indeed, becomes almost a trade mark of Eve's, a characteristic
by which we come to recognize her speeches. But the relationship between
Adam and Eve is not one in which the dependence is all one way. Adam,
though in different, less formal ways, is shown to be equally dependent on
her. The recurrent image of the Garden that is associated with them is the
traditional one of the vine and the elm; without the elm the vine lacks
support, but without the vine the elm is "barren". Thus

> On their morning's rural work they haste,
> Among sweet dews and flowers; where any row
> Of fruit trees over-woody reached too far
> Their pampered boughs, and needed hands to check
> Fruitless embraces: or they led the vine
> To wed her elm; she spoused about him twines
> Her marriageable arms, and with her brings
> Her dower the adopted clusters, to adorn
> His barren leaves . . .   (V, 211–19)

And the dependence of Adam on Eve is made clear in a most important
scene in which he pleads with God for her creation. Adam thanks God for
the liberality with which He has provided for his needs in the Garden;
"But with me" he says,

> I see not who partakes. In solitude
> What happiness, who can enjoy alone,
> Or all enjoying, what contentment find?   (VIII, 364–66)

God, who here inclines toward playfulness, suggests that Adam has all the
creatures of the Garden as his companions, to which Adam responds in
what may be seen as Milton's statement of his ideal of the marriage
relationship:

> Hast thou not made me here thy substitute,
> And these inferior far beneath me set?
> Among unequals what society
> Can sort, what harmony or true delight?
> Which must be mutual, in proportion due
> Given and received; but, in disparity
> The one intense, the other still remiss
> Cannot well suit with either, but soon prove

> Tedious alike: of fellowship I speak
> Such as I seek, fit to participate
> all rational delight . . .   (VIII, 381−91)

If this does indeed reflect Milton's view of marriage, it suggests that he was not altogether the male chauvinist he has sometimes been dubbed, that he gave to women, in fact, a role in marriage which they did not generally achieve before the twentieth century. It may be that the failure of his own marriage resulted simply from the fact that he expected too much of his wife. To be expected to "participate / All rational delight" with a man of Milton's accomplishments could well be a terrifying prospect for any person, let alone a girl with the kind of education typically allowed to women in Milton's day. But to return to the poem, once again God counters with the suggestion that Adam wants something which He (God), "who am alone from all eternity", lacks. To which Adam replies that

> Thou in thyself art perfect, and in thee
> Is no deficience found not so is man.   (VIII, 415−16)

Thus God has manouevred Adam into admitting that he needs Eve, that without her he is incomplete, and He is now willing to admit that He had all along intended to provide Adam with a companion. He had, however, wished to have Adam realize that her creation was in accordance with his own wishes, and not something foisted on him, as it were, from above − a sensible precaution as can be seen after the fall when Adam blames God for the whole thing by virtue of His having created Eve. For the moment, however,

> What next I bring shall please thee, be assured,
> Thy likeness, thy fit help, thy other self,
> Thy wish exactly to thy heart's desire.   (VIII, 449−51)

We shall need to return later to the continuance of this scene, where Adam reveals to Raphael the effect that Eve has on him. But it might be noted here that there does seem to be some discrepancy between what Adam asked for − a creature "fit to participate / All rational delight" − and what he in fact got − one who seems rather to destroy the very basis of his rationality. As he tells Raphael:

> All higher knowledge in her presence falls
> Degraded, wisdom in discourse with her
> Loses discountenanced, and like folly shows.   (VIII, 551−53)

Again, in the description we are given of the pair in our first introduction to them, Eve may not seem to be exactly what Adam was expecting:

> For contemplation he and valour formed,
> For softness she and sweet attractive grace.   (IV, 297−98)

But Milton's Eve is far too complex, her image far too dependent on a multitude of often apparently minor detail for her to be summed up in any simple way. She is an elusive, disturbing creation, alongside the steady dependability of her husband. By contrast with Adam's essentially well-ordered appearance,

> She as a veil down to the slender waist
> Her unadorned golden tresses wore
> Dishevelled, but in wanton ringlets waved.   (IV, 304—6)

This epithet "wanton" is characteristic of the apparently "fallen" images that pursue Eve through the poem; while retaining its primary meaning of disordered luxuriance, it inevitably introduces more disturbing connotations. And "dishevelled" appears innocuous enough, unless one thinks forward to the dream which Satan induces in Eve, when Adam awakes to find her "With tresses discomposed, and glowing cheek" (V, 10).

Eve, whose "Beauty, which whether waking or asleep, / Shot forth peculiar graces" (V, 14—15), is indeed a disturbing influence in the supposedly perfect order and harmony of the Garden; and it seems not altogether inconsequential that she should be associated in simile and metaphor with so many famous and often destructive women, heroines and goddesses of story and legend — Pandora, Diana, Proserpina, Hera, Helen, Venus — albeit the association is characteristically a negative one:

> What day the genial angel to our sire
> Brought her in naked beauty more adorned,
> More lovely than Pandora . . .   (IV, 712—14)

The association remains imaginatively, as the poet recognizes almost immediately: "O! too like / In sad event . . . when . . . she ensnared / Mankind with her fair looks". And the same complex image is presented in the very first view that we — and Satan (it is suggestive that we never see Eve except when Satan or his influence is present) — the first view that we have of Eve, when she is associated with the image of Proserpina:

> . . . Not that fair field
> Of Enna, where Proserpine gathering flowers,
> Her self a fairer flower by gloomy Dis
> Was gathered, which cost Ceres all that pain
> To seek her through the world. . . .   (IV, 268—72)

In this image are prefigured both Eve's beauty and the misfortune which this beauty brings on herself and on man; and the effect of the image is heightened if we remember that the capture of Proserpina resulted in her alliance with the potentate of Hell. The fact that neither the pagan Hell nor its king quite parallels the Christian variety tends to be overlooked. Eve's resolution after she has eaten the apple is thus already at this first moment prepared for, "Adam shall share with me in bliss or woe" (IX, 831). The paradox of Eve is heightened, too, by her also being constantly referred to throughout the poem in her relationship to the second Eve, Mary, the mother of Christ, whose "virgin seed" is finally "to bruise the heel" of Satan. Her associations thus are those of both destroyer and saviour of man, of seductress and virgin mother; and these associations inform the image of unfallen sexuality which is also part of our vision of her in her "subjection" to Adam:

> . . . by her yielded, by him best received,
> Yielded with coy submission, modest pride,
> And sweet reluctant amorous delay.   (IV, 309—11)

Our impression of the two comes more into focus as we listen to them talk together. For Adam the Garden is a pleasant place, but one which primarily makes practical demands on him. They should retire early, he says, because,

> Tomorrow ere fresh morning streak the east
> With first approach of light, we must be risen,
> And at our pleasant labour, to reform
> Yon flowery arbours, yonder alleys green,
> Our walk at noon with branches overgrown,
> That mock our scant manuring . . .
> Mean while, as nature wills, night bids us rest.   (IV, 623—33)

But for Eve the Garden is a place of beauty, and in contrast to Adam's pedestrian words she responds to it in poetry that is ordered, stylized, ceremonious, yet still sensuous — a sensuousness in which she seeks to involve Adam:

> With thee conversing I forget all time,
> All seasons and their change, all please alike.
> Sweet is the breath of morn, her rising sweet,
> With charm of earliest birds; pleasant the sun,
> When first on this delightful land he spreads
> His orient beams, on herb, tree, fruit, and flower,
> Glistering with dew; fragrant the fertile earth
> After soft showers . . .
> But neither breath of Morn . . .
> Nor grateful evening mild, nor silent night
> With this her solemn bird, nor walk by moon,
> Or glittering starlight without thee is sweet.   (IV, 639—56)

From passages like this it becomes increasingly apparent that Adam's strength is in his logical, rather scientific turn of mind, and his tendency is to become preoccupied with purely pragmatic concerns. By comparison with Eve he is less given to spontaneity, inventiveness or flights of imagination — unless instigated by the influence of Eve — although it is true that on astronomical matters his roving curiosity earns him a rebuke from Raphael to "Solicit not thy thoughts with matters hid, / Leave them to

God above" (VIII, 167—68). Eve is weaker than Adam in reason and stronger in imaginative capacity. On the anagogical level of the poem — though this is never allowed to come to the surface, Adam and Eve remaining at all times human rather than allegorical characters — on the anagogical level the relationship is such that from it comes an adrogynous soul composed of the "masculine" quality of reason represented by Adam, and the "feminine" quality of creative imagination which Eve embodies. Adam expounds this concept in his attempt to interpret Eve's dream:

> . . . But know that in the soul
> Are many lesser faculties that serve
> Reason as chief. Among these fancy next
> Her office holds; of all external things,
> Which the five watchful senses represent,
> She forms imaginations, airy shapes,
> Which reason joining or disjoining, frames
> All what we affirm or what deny, and call
> Our knowledge or opinion . . .   (V, 100—108)

This explanation is limited by its being tied to the psychological theory available to Milton in the seventeenth century, but it does explain the keen receptivity to sensual stimulation that is evident in Eve's aesthetic response to the Garden. It is the fancy's role to collect and collate data from the senses; it is the reason's role to approve or reject the fancy's creation — as on various occasions we see Adam doing in response to Eve's enthusiasms. And Eve's sensual response to things is reflected and further defined by the response of others towards her: Adam's, of course, and also Satan's, whom she "sweetly rapes" of his evil intent just before his temptation of her:

> Such pleasure took the serpent to behold
> This flowery plat, the sweet recess of Eve
> Thus early, thus alone; her heavenly form
> Angelic, but more soft and feminine,
> Her graceful innocence, her every air
> Of gesture or least action overawed
> His malice, and with sweet rapine bereaved
> His fierceness of the fierce intent it brought.   (IX, 455—62)

Eve, however, is not simply a beauty queen. Milton is sufficiently mindful of her as his concept of the ideal wife for this not to be so. Thus when Adam seeks to enter into an astronomical discussion with Raphael, and "by his countenance seemed / Entering on studious thoughts abstruse", Eve leaves them together to go out among her plants and flowers:

> Yet went she not, as not with such discourse
> Delighted, or not capable her ear
> Of what was high. Such pleasure she reserved,

Adam relating, she sole auditress;
Her husband the relater she preferred
Before the angel, and of him to ask
Chose rather ...   (VIII, 48–54)

Raphael, indeed, underestimates both her and Adam when rebuking Adam
for allowing his reason to be unduly influenced by her beauty. "For what
admir'st thou" he asks,

... what transports thee so?
An outside? Fair no doubt, and worthy well
Thy cherishing, thy honouring, and thy love;
Not thy subjection ...   (VIII, 567–70)

Raphael is right to the extent that Adam is in danger of placing Eve in
God's place; but he goes too far in attributing her effect on him purely to
her physical beauty. It is not, Adam replies, "her outside formed so fair"

So much delights me as those graceful acts,
Those thousand decencies, that daily flow
From all her words and actions mixed with love
And sweet compliance, which declare unfeigned
Union of mind, or in us both one soul,
Harmony to behold in wedded pair.   (VIII, 600–605)

Milton's Eve is indeed a worthy wife for Adam and worthy of her central
role in man's struggle with evil.

This then is what Eve is; but the more important question is not what
she is but what she does, what her role is in the story of the fall. The
central act of that role is, of course, determined by Milton's source. It was
Eve according to the Genesis story who first ate the apple and there was
no way that Milton could, or would have wanted to, alter this. What he
had to do was to make her act imaginatively acceptable and understandable, and we have already seen, in the slight but unmistakably disturbing
influence of her presence in the Garden, something of how he moves to do
this: her "wanton tresses", the "darts of desire" which shoot from her, her
"peculiar graces" in a world in which harmony rather than individuality is
or should be dominant.

The first decisively significant episode, however, is that of Eve's earliest
conscious moments after her creation, when her sensuous response to
beauty – in this case her own – as she catches sight of her reflection in a
pool, involves her in a parallel to the Narcissus story and provides an
indication of the tendency to self-love, to self-pride, on which Satan is
later to work his wiles. More definite is the incident already referred to,
her response to the beauty, this time of the Garden. Her expression of this
response ends as she asks the significant question:

But wherefore all night long shine these, for whom
This glorious sight, when sleep hath shut all eyes?   (IV, 657–58)

Again here is the tendency, innocent but significant, towards self-pride, towards seeing herslef as the centre of reference, seeing her own awareness as giving meaning to everything around her. It is part of the poem's presentation of the Christian-humanist paradox that its effect as a whole, as we discussed earlier, is to place man in just this central position. But on the more immediate, "formal" level Eve is wrong to see herself in this position, and Adam corrects her; but it has to be remembered that Satan is also present, lurking in the undergrowth, seeking ways of attacking Adam and Eve. That Eve's potentiality for self-pride does not escape him is soon apparent. After Adam and Eve retire for the night he is discovered by the scouts of Gabriel "squat like a toad, close at the ear of Eve" (IV, 800), and his influence is apparent in the dream of which Eve tells Adam in the morning. "Methought" she says,

> Close at mine ear one called me forth to walk
> With gentle voice, I thought it thine . . .   (V, 36—37)

But the words the voice speaks are clearly not those of the practical, unimaginative Adam; rather they are Eve's own — or Satan speaking to her with her own voice, her own stylized, ceremonious but still sensuous response to beauty:

> Why sleep'st thou Eve? Now is the pleasant time,
> The cool, the silent, save where silence yields
> To the night-warbling bird, that now awake
> Tunes sweetest his love-laboured song . . .   (V, 38—41)

The voice concludes by answering Eve's question from the night before:

> . . . heaven wakes with all his eyes;
> Whom to behold but thee, nature's desire,
> In whose sight all things joy, with ravishment
> Attracted by thy beauty still to gaze.   (V, 44—47)

And the dream that follows may be seen as going beyond the invitation to simple sensuousness or self-pride, to suggest something like sexual excitement:

> So saying, he drew nigh, and to me held,
> Even to my mouth, of that same fruit held part
> Which he had plucked; the pleasant savoury smell
> So quickened appetite, that I, methought,
> Could not but taste. Forthwith up to the clouds
> With him I flew . . .
> . . . suddenly
> My guide was gone, and I, me thought, sunk down,
> And fell asleep . . .   (V, 82—92)

We shall need to remember this suggestion of sexuality in our consideration of the fall itself. First, however, there are two other important passages which have already been mentioned but which need further consideration for the central role that Eve plays in them. The first concerns Adam's response to Eve's creation. Adam is here speaking of an event which he shared directly with God and his form of speech is reminiscent of Eve's when speaking to him, which, of course, is as it should be since for her *he* is in the place of God. Thus he begins "correctly":

> . . . well I understand in the prime end
> Of nature her the inferior, in the mind
> And inward faculties, which most excel;
> In outward also her resembling less
> His image who made both . . .   (VIII, 540–44)

But then the tone changes and the voice sounds very much more like Eve's:

> . . . yet when I approach
> Her loveliness, so absolute she seems
> And in herself complete, so well to know
> Her own, that what she wills to do or say
> Seems wisest, virtuousest, discreetest, best.   (VIII, 546–50)

Adam of course is being absolutely wrong here. Only moments before he has said that God alone is complete in himself, but now he claims the same for Eve; and he goes on in a passage quoted earlier to say that under her influence "all higher knowledge . . . falls degraded". Yet I think that most readers will none the less find the Adam revealed in these lines more attractive than the dull, practical, somewhat priggish character he has hitherto largely appeared to be. He becomes, indeed, for the first time genuinely human, suggesting the real significance of his need for Eve – that without her he is somehow less than human, lacking the imagination, the sensitivity, which is her special contribution to the human psyche. In this key passage, then, Eve's dual role is defined. She is what is needed in order to complete man, that without which he is less than human; but she is also his danger, his weakness, the influence that distracts him and draws him away from an understanding of the truth, away from what is to what seems to be.

In the movement towards the fall Eve's role has thus far been no more than a possible influence, a potential danger. At the beginning of Book IX, when the fall draws near and Milton must "change his notes to tragic", Eve's part becomes more decisive. If man is to fail it must not be the result of chance but the result of a deliberate wrong choice on his part, and Milton extends this to include the circumstances which allow Satan to attack Eve while she is separated from Adam. The quarrel, or slight domestic tiff, which leads to Eve parting from Adam to garden alone has already been discussed as part of the consideration of Eve's freedom. What is important to recognize here is that the fall is from this point of view an example of what may happen when whatever it is that Eve represents insists on its independence and endeavours to act alone, separated from what is represented by Adam; when Eve, to use the strain of imagery that persists throughout the treatment of her relationship with Adam, becomes the " . . . fairest unsupported flower, / From her best prop so far" (IX, 432—33).

At its simplest level, Satan's temptation of Eve can be seen as based on those tendencies to self-love and self-pride, to seeing herself as the centre of importance, that we have already discussed. Thus Satan addresses her as

> Fairest resemblance of thy maker fair,
> Thee all things living gaze on, all things thine
> By gift, and thy celestial beauty adore
> With ravishment beheld, there best beheld
> Where universally admired . . .   (IX, 538—42)

But we may also remember Adam's confession to Raphael that "apt the mind or fancy is to rove / Unchecked, and of her roving is no end" (VIII, 188—89). This is a response to Raphael's injunction to "be lowly wise: / Think only what concerns thee and thy being" (VIII, 173—74), and Adam is applying it to himself. But we may feel that Eve with her more spontaneous response to the wonder of things may be more liable even than Adam to fall into this sort of error, to respond more readily to Satan when he claims to:

> . . . have touched and tasted, yet both live,
> And life more perfect have attained than fate
> Meant me, by venturing higher than my lot.   (IX, 688—90)

Satan is indeed seeking to attack Eve through her "aspiring mind", and after eating the apple she claims to "grow mature / In knowledge, as the gods who all things know" (IX, 803—804). Eve at this point is very much the Faustus figure, selling herself to the Devil in return for superhuman power and knowledge.

There is also the matter of the sexual significance noted in the earlier dream which may help put the serpent's invitation to eat into the context of an invitation to widen experience through adultery:

> . . . one man except,
> Who sees thee? (And what is one?) Who shouldst be seen
> A goddess among gods . . .   (IX, 545—47)

Looked at in this way the fall may be seem as stemming from Eve's desire towards the exploration specifically of her own sexuality, that part of herself that basically distinguishes her from Adam. Which in turn may cause us to look back at the two occasions on which Satan enters the Garden. First he leaps over the wall and like a thief in the night steals into Eve's thoughts. But on the second occasion, immediately prior to the temptation of Eve, we are told of a place where

Rose up a fountain by the tree of life;
In with the river sunk, and with it rose,
Satan . . .   (IX, 73–75)

We have already noted the suggestion from this that evil enters life at
its very source, but its proximity to the temptation of Eve may give it
further implications. By falling to Satan, Eve takes death into herself.
She becomes the great paradox, the source of life as well as death, and
the words applied to Chaos could well be applied to her: the "womb of
nature, or perhaps her grave" (II, 911). The opening of the womb which
should correspond to the gates of paradise becomes instead, as in the
allegory of Sin in Book II, a hell-mouth producing fodder for death. In
this role Eve is an image of the paradoxes and tensions of sexuality in the
fallen world, the desire to reproduce and create life in one's own image
and thereby to experience something of death.

The fall as it concerns Adam I shall deal with elsewhere. I want here,
however, to point to the way in which the responses of Adam and Eve
respectively to the fall are nicely contrasted, giving a beautifully balanced
structure to this section of the poem. As regards Eve we have already seen
in an earlier essay how she is at her worst, at her moral nadir, immediately
after eating the apple; how her first thought is to seek an advantage over
Adam by keeping the experience from him, until the dreadful thought
strikes her that God may "have seen", and that in consequence she will
die. Then, "A death to think", Adam may be wedded to another Eve,
while she is "extinct". No, she resolves, "Adam shall share with me in
bliss or woe", and she ends with the extraordinary hypocrisy of:

So dear I love him, that with him all deaths
I could endure, without him live no life.   (IX, 832–33)

Adam, by contrast, at the moment of his fall is for most readers at his
most sympathetic as he delivers a beautifully lyric expression of love for
Eve, undoubted in its sincerity. Afterwards they share the feelings first
of lust then of the shame and mutual recrimination that follow; but from
there, while Eve begins the slow upward climb towards redemption, for
Adam the degeneration continues. Their reversed moral positions are
clearly reflected in their responses when the Son comes to the Garden
as their judge. Both are ashamed and hide among the trees. When eventually they are brought out to face their accuser Adam's words indicate
none of the nobility of his utterances to Eve at the actual time of the fall:

O heaven! in evil strait this day I stand
Before my judge, either to undergo
My self the total crime, or to accuse
My other self, the partner of my life
Whose failing, while her faith to me remains,
I should conceal, and not expose to blame

By my complaint; but strict necessity
Subdues me . . .
. . . should I hold my peace, yet thou
Wouldst easily detect what I conceal.
This woman whom thou madest to be my help
and gavest me as thy perfect gift, so good,

.   .   .   .   .
That from her hand I could suspect no ill,

.   .   .   .   .
She gave me of the tree, and I did eat.   (X, 125–43)

In contrast to this tissue of excuses, Eve's brief reply is a model of dignity:

The serpent me beguiled and I did eat.   (X, 162)

Adam's moral degeneration continues, to culminate in a long soliloquy,
the longest in the poem, strongly reminiscent of Satan's outburst at the
beginning of Book III, thus revealing to what Satanic depths Adam has
now sunk. Increasingly through the speech he puts the blame on Eve, and
he ends with a violent attack on women and on marriage,

Which infinite calamity shall cause
To human life, and household peace confound.   (X, 907–8)

But this is not, as it is liable to be read, an expression of Milton's own
views, deriving from his own allegedly unfortunate marital experiences.
On the contrary, he exalts marriage and women by making Adam's deroga-
tion of them a sign of the moral degeneration he has undergone, just as he
uses the wedding bower as the very centre of their bliss and innocence.
The attack has its dramatic purpose, too, leading as it does by contrast
immediately into Eve's finest moment when, in what are perhaps the most
beautiful lines of the poem, she seeks to take on herself the role of the
redeemer, sacrificing herself for Adam:

Forsake me not thus, Adam! witness heaven
What love sincere and reverence in my heart
I bear thee, and unweeting have offended,
Unhappily deceived . . .
. . . Forlorn of thee
Whither shall I betake me, where subsist?
While yet we live, scarce one short hours perhaps,
Between us two let there be peace . . .
. . . On me exercise not
Thy hatred for this misery befallen,
On me already lost, me than thyself
More miserable. Both have sinned; but thou
Against God only, I against God and thee,
And to the place of judgement will return,
There with my cries importune heaven, that all
The sentence from thy head removed may light

On me, sole cause to thee of all this woe,
Me me only just object of his ire.   (X, 914—36)

Adam rebukes her in terms that are not altogether gracious. "Bear thine own [guilt] first" he tells her, "ill able to sustain / His full wrath thou feel'st as yet least part, / And my displeasure bear'st so ill" (X, 950—52). But Eve's words have had their effect and he turns from his selfish obsessions with a plea that they should

  . . . strive
In offices of love how we may lighten
Each other's burden in our share of woe.   (X, 959—61)

This return to unselfishness results in a renewal of their ability to speak to God in prayer, and is thus a first step in breaking down that alienation from God that was the fundamental outcome of the fall. Thus Eve maintains her role. Just as she is necessary to complete Adam while at the same time making it possible for him to be destroyed, so having brought about that destruction she is also the means towards his redemption.

In this role Eve captures the paradox of Christ, the "female" side of God, willing to die for mankind, that manifestation of God that reconciles the Old and New Testaments. Eve's fall and dramatic rise can thus be seen in terms of Christ's harrowing of Hell, or — going back to an earlier image associated with her — to Proserpina's time spent in the underworld, while at the same time demonstrating the height of vision sometimes reached by the imagination. Raphael, in attempting to depict the working of Heaven, commented on the difficulty of raising "Human imagination to such highth / Of Godlike power" (VI, 300—301), but Eve reaches this height through love, and in doing so captures something of the intuitive vision of the angels. Carried up by inspiration, by "internal" (VIII, 461) or "mental" (XI, 418) sight, she reaches the exhilarating peaks of poetic inspiration.

For Eve the final two books of the poem represent a consolidation of her role. The scene in which Michael pronounces their sentence of banishment from the Garden provides an opportunity for a restatement of her relationship with Adam. Eve's response to the thought of going is one to the loss of the Garden itself:

  . . . O flowers,
That never will in other climate grow,
My early visitation, and my last
At even, which I bred up with tender hand
From the first opening bud, and gave ye names.   (XI, 273—77)

Michael's consolation for her is that even without the Garden she still has Adam:

Thy going is not lonely; with thee goes
Thy husband, him to follow thou art bound.   (XI, 290—91)

For Adam, however, the loss is not one of the Garden itself but of it as a place where he has known God:

> This most afflicts me, that departing hence,
> As from his face I shall be hid, deprived
> His blessed countenance . . .   (XI, 315–17)

And for him Michael's consolation is that God is not to be known only in the Garden:

> Adam, thou know'st heaven his, and all the earth,
> Not this rock only . . .
> . . . surmise not, then
> His presence to these narrow bounds confined
> Of Paradise or Eden . . .   (XI, 335–42)

Thus, as I have said, the basic pattern of their relationship, affirmed on our very first meeting with them, is re-established:

> He for God only, she for God in him.   (IV, 299)

They are now able to leave the Garden once more "hand in hand".

Before they do so, however, Eve is herself allowed to realize her dual role as destroyer and yet preserver of mankind. At the end of his narration to Adam of events to come, Michael instructs him to tell Eve particularly "what may concern her faith to know / The great deliverance by her seed to come" (XII, 599–600). And the last words we hear from Adam and Eve are given to her to express her consciousness of her role:

> . . . but now lead on;
> In me is no delay; with thee to go,
> Is to stay here; without thee here to stay
> Is to go hence unwilling; thou to me
> Art all things under heaven, all places thou,
> Who for my wilful crime art banished hence.
> This further consolation yet secure
> I carry hence: though all by me is lost,
> Such favour I unworthy am vouchsafed,
> By me the promised seed shall all restore.   (XII, 614–23)

It is perhaps significant that in *Paradise Regained* Mary, the second Eve, has almost no role, except to sit at home and wait, while her son, God made man, is left to struggle alone against the power of evil. But that is the subject of a later essay.

6

The War in Heaven

The account of the war in Heaven as it is given by Raphael to Adam is one of the most puzzling and to many readers the least successful episodes in *Paradise Lost*. On first reading the whole business may seem rather ridiculous and to be accounted for only in terms of Raphael's initial question to Adam: " . . . how shall I relate / To human sense the invisible exploits / Of warring Spirits?". To which he provides his own answer, that

> . . . what surmounts the reach
> Of human sense, I shall delineate so,
> By likening spiritual to corporeal forms
> As may express them best . . .   (V, 571–74)

The ridiculousness then is seen as coming from Raphael's attempts to bring spiritual phenomena within the reach of human understanding; although he does go on to suggest that Earth may be "but the shadow of heaven, and things therein / Each to other like, more than on earth is thought" (V, 575–76). But on closer examination the events of the war become much more complex in their significance than this. Raphael's narrative is no more simply a dramatic representation of the rebellion of Satan than *Paradise Lost* as a whole is a simple story of the fall of Adam and Eve.

The figure of God is central to the whole episode and ostensibly He seems to manipulate and direct the events with an immediacy that is not typical of His part in other events of the story. The return of Abdiel from Satan's quarters in the north where the rebellion has been hatched and where he alone has stood out against Satan may be taken as the actual beginning of hostilities. He is greeted by God with:

> Servant of God, well done, well hast thou fought
> The better fight, who single hast maintained
> Against revolted multitudes the cause
> Of truth, in word mightier than they in arms;
> And for the testimony of truth hast borne
> Universal reproach, far worse to bear
> Than violence . . .   (VI, 29–35)

The power of truth is thus set up as triumphant, as the "better fight", against the violence of armed might. But immediately God seems to turn to just that armed might for defence against the rebels:

> Go Michael of celestial armies prince,
> And thou in military prowess next
> Gabriel lead forth to battle these my sons
> Invincible, lead forth my armed saints,
> By thousands and by millions ranged for fight;
> Equal in number to that godless crew
> Rebellious . . .   (VI, 44—50)

Indeed, even before Abdiel's return God had spoken to the Son of their need to defend themselves:

> Nearly it now concerns us to be sure
> Of our omnipotence, and with what arms
> We mean to hold what anciently we claim
> Of diety or empire . . .
> Let us advise, and to this hazard draw
> With speed what force is left, and all employ
> In our defence, lest unawares we lose
> This our high place, our sanctuary, our hill.   (V, 721—32)

But this of course is ironic. It is ridiculous that the omnipotent God should be caught napping, as it were, and pushed off His hill; and the Son recognizes the irony of it:

> . . . Mighty Father, thou thy foes
> Justly hast in derision and secure
> Laugh'st at their vain designs and tumults vain.   (VI, 735—37)

Satan's whole enterprise is ridiculous from the beginning. The omnipotent God cannot be overthrown, least of all by strength of arms. But why in that case, recognizing it as ridiculous, does God react in the way He does, sending Michael and the armed host of Heaven to meet the challenge. Particularly when He must know that the task in this form is beyond them, that only Christ with the power of perfect truth and goodness can achieve victory; when He knows from the start that the only possible result of the battle between the good and bad angels is stalemate and farce, that "in perpetual fight they needs must last / Endless, and no solution will be found" (VI, 693—94). Against this knowledge, His orders to Michael and Gabriel to

> . . . them with fire and hostile arms
> Fearless assault; and to the brow of heaven
> Pursuing, drive them out from God and bliss
> Into their place of punishment . . .   (VI, 50—53)

must be just as ironic as His first mocking reaction to the rebellion, although one may object that there is a difference between ironic comment and the sending out of an army to fight in a spirit of irony.

Milton was, of course, writing against a background of relatively recent civil war in England and part of his purpose almost certainly was to show the futility of such war, that it settles nothing. But this is an additional benefit rather than a sufficient explanation of his manner of treating the war in Heaven. Before going further, however, it is necessary to remember that the account of the war is provided not by the divinely inspired narrator but by Raphael; that even the words of God are in this case repeated through Raphael. For this reason nothing in the narrative is necessarily to be taken absolutely at its face value. And if it is shown that the war in Heaven is in a sense an example of imperfect understanding, on the part of the good angels as well as the bad, of the nature of God's moral law in relation to evil, Raphael as one of those involved could well be regarded as fallible. One point on which this fallibility might be seen to occur is that of the perspective and role of God. Throughout *Paradise Lost* Milton's God is not a being or an active character in the same way, for instance, that Satan is, though at times He may appear to be. He is the sum total of the moral law, and as such His function is simply to state that law. His position in relation to the war in Heaven parallels that in relation to the fall of Adam and Eve. His foreknowledge of both does not imply any direction or manipulation of events. Thus God has no actual part in the action of the war, any more than He has in the action of the fall; He is not the celestial strategist who has made a tactical error by sending Michael and his troops into a battle they cannot win, as appears in Raphael's narrative. Events follow an inevitable course which He in no way acts to cause or prevent.

Seen in this way the intervention of Michael and his followers, like the fall of man, is to be seen, not as directed by God, but as psychologically determined, the immediate reaction of the forces of good to the eruption of evil. And the war in Heaven becomes an image of misguided energy, a contest in which the participants have only a limited understanding of the working of the forces, moral and physical, involved. And to this extent the good angels serve as symbols for the state of man himself, struggling to oppose evil yet uncertain of the most appropriate or successful means of doing so. Paradoxically the war in Heaven is in many ways a very human episode, part of the continuing human reference of the whole poem, and thus of more immediate relevance as part of Raphael's warning to Adam than it might at first seem to be.

In developing this complex image of the war in Heaven Milton follows what for him is a typical strategy of setting up comfortable expectations in the reader which are then more and more upset. Raphael's narrative of the rebellion begins clearly enough, within a recognizably epic framework and a pattern of imagery that emphasizes the negative nature of the revolt as against the positive nature of the angelic response. Satan's revolt, like the fall of man, is a transgression of the central concept of hierarchy, on which the order of God's universe depends. Sin, as the transgression of this order, brings with it disorder, discord, chaos and disharmony. Throughout the poem Milton emphasizes that sin is fundamentally uncreative or anti-creative, since it opposes the natural order of creation and it is fitting, therefore, that the event which precipitates Satan's revolt is the elevation of the Son as part of that creative order to a position next to God:

> This day I have begot whom I declare
> My only Son, and on this holy hill
> Him have anointed...   (V, 603—5)

In contrast to the spontaneous joy and perfect harmony of the angels' response to this event, Satan hatches his plot under cover of night and darkness, symbols of chaos and uncreation, and quickly surrounds himself with an aura of distrust and deceit. "More in this place" he tells his henchman, "To utter is not safe" (V, 682—83), and he leads his followers to the "north" — itself a symbol of darkness and sterility — on the pretext of preparing a "fit entertainment to receive our King".

It is here that there occurs the first interruption to what is to be the purely epic — that is, "heroic" in the traditional sense — development of the narrative, as Abdiel emerges as the first of the "few faithful men", the so-called types of Christ:

> So spake the seraph Abdiel faithful found;
> Among the faithless, faithful only he;
> Among innumerable false, unmoved,
> Unshaken, unseduced, unterrified
> His loyalty he kept, his love, his zeal;
> Nor number, nor example with him wrought
> To swerve from truth, or change his constant mind
> Though single ...   (V, 896—903)

Abdiel's simple individual rejection of evil from a basis of personal faith and integrity is the real alternative to the spurious activity of physical warfare as a means of establishing the victory of good over evil. To put faith in the latter course, to believe that the moral force of evil can be met with the physical force of arms, is to make a Satanic blunder about the nature of morality, a blunder perpetuated in the never-ending "holy wars" that have marked human progress through the centuries. The true meaning of the image of the triumphant Christ at the end of Book VI as he single handedly drives the rebels from Heaven is a re-establishment of the personal locus of morality that we see in the figure of Abdiel.

In the meanwhile, however, as we have seen, the faithful angels react as men have continued to do ever since and put their faith in the big battalions, in the "millions ranged for fight / Equal in number to that godless crew", so certain that God is on their side that they believe Him actually to have ordered them into battle. And just as wars, at least in their beginnings, have continued to men to seem glorious, the enthusiasm of the good angels — even though it is misplaced — their obedience to what they see as the will of God and their belief in the righteousness of their cause, strike us too as glorious. The imagery of light and brightness that surrounds them places them in stark contrast to the darkness of the rebel forces:

> ... thick embattled squadrons bright,
> Chariots and flaming arms, and fiery steeds
> Reflecting blaze on blaze ... (VI, 16—18)

And as they march off to their holy war they are portrayed in terms of order and harmony:

> ... the powers militant
> That stood for heaven, in mighty quadrate joined
> Of union irresistible, moved on
> In silence their bright legions, to the sound
> Of instrumental harmony, that breathed
> Heroic ardour to adventurous deeds. (VI, 61—66)

The sense of a graceful, ordered advance in these lines contrasts sharply with the "furious expedition" of the rebels:

> Bristled with upright beams innumerable
> Of rigid spears, and helmets thronged, and shields
> Various, with boastful argument portrayed,
> The banded powers of Satan hasting on
> With furious expedition ... (VI, 82—86)

Similarly the advance of the good angels "high above the ground" (VI, 71) leads Raphael to refer by way of analogy to the naming of the birds by Adam immediately after his creation; and this reference serves not only to remind the reader that Adam is listening — to re-establish the dramatic situation — but also to associate Michael's legions in his, and Adam's, mind with the positive values of divine creativeness.

Once the two angelic forces meet on the battlefield, this positive—negative polarity between the two sides begins to break down, as the complex moral aspects of the image begin to be more apparent and both sides are increasingly revealed as limited in their understanding of the true nature of the moral conflict. Abdiel is again a central figure in this development. Previously seen as the single individual opposed to the mass hysteria whipped up by Satan's rhetoric, Abdiel is now subsumed in the collective attempt to overcome evil by physical force; is now himself, as it were, one of the mob. The first ominous signs of an imperfect intuition of the nature of evil come when he sees Satan and is amazed that his powerful and awe-inspiring appearance has not changed as a result of his rejection of God:

> O heaven! That such resemblance of the highest
> Should yet remain, where faith and realty
> Remain not . . .   (VI, 114–16)

This betrays at least some ignorance of evil, of its subtlety and incipient attractiveness, and thus despite his former stand on simple faith it is not altogether unexpected when Abdiel goes on to show his involvement in the confusion of moral and physical force that is seen to be involving all the angelic host. "His puissance", he says,

> . . . trusting in th'almighty's aid,
> I mean to try, whose reason I have tried
> Unsound and false; nor is it aught but just
> That he who in debate of truth hath won
> Should win in arms, in both disputes alike
> Victor.   (VI, 119–24)

Against this background of his own statement Abdiel's taunt:

> . . . fool, not to think how vain
> Against the omnipotent to rise in arms . . .   (VI, 135–36)

becomes ironic. He is himself equally foolish, even if more laudable, in seeking *on behalf of* "the omnipotent to rise in arms".

The account of Satan's wounding by first Abdiel and then Michael serves to help build the complex image of the war and its relation to the corresponding image of evil. Satan's fallen dependence on, and misguided faith in, the physical and material over the absolute truth of the moral and spiritual is obvious throughout the whole episode, but his wounding serves both to show the ludicrous absurdity of this tendency and also to involve the good angels in it as well. When Michael wounds Satan, the confusion of spirit and matter makes for real comic incongruity:

> The griding sword with discontinuous wound
> Passed through him, but the ethereal substance closed
> Not long divisible, and from the gash
> A stream of nectarous humour issuing flowed
> Sanguine, such as celestial spirits may bleed,
> And all his armour stained, erewhile so bright.   (VI, 329–34)

This is farcical and it makes Satan ridiculous. One is reminded of the fun that Pope made of it in the "battle of the sexes" in his mock-heroic masterpiece, *The Rape of the Lock*, when one of the sylphs interposed itself to prevent the cutting off of Belinda's hair and got itself cut in two for its pains: "But airy spirits soon unite again". And the ridicule also pertains to the inflictor of the wound, since the action is so absurdly ineffective. Certainly Satan then "first knew pain" but this does not render the action of Michael effective, because it is clear that Satan's pain is ultimately self-inflicted, the result of his own sin. That this is so is indicated by the fact that the only difference between the good and the bad angels is the tendency of the latter alone to feel pain. As the battle reaches its height, the Satanic host

> Then first with fear surprised and sense of pain
> Fled ignominious, to such evil brought
> By sin of disobedience, till that hour
> Not liable to fear or flight or pain.
> Far otherwise the inviolable Saints
>
> .   .   .   .   .
> Such high advantages their innocence
> Gave them above their foes, not to have sinned
> Not to have disobeyed; in fight they stood
> Unwearied, unobnoxious to be pained
> By wound, though from their place by violence moved.
>   (VI, 394—405)

By seeking physically to wound Satan, then, Michael here shows himself liable to the Satanic tendency to materialistic self-deception through his misguided attempt to defeat evil by force; and it is interesting that under later and less pressing circumstances Michael corrects Adam for just the same mistake, telling him that it is not by any "local wounds / Of head or heel" that evil is finally to be defeated (XII, 385—91). And in this action with Satan Michael may also be seen to share with him the Satanic sin of pride, expressed in the belief of each in his physical prowess, which overrides any consciousness of the moral mistake each is involved in:

> Together both, with next to almighty arm
> Uplifted imminent one stroke they aimed
> That might determine, and not need repeat.   (VI, 316—18)

From the perspective of God, Michael and Satan, along with the host of both good and bad angels, exhibit the phenomenon of "strength from truth divided" (VI, 381), and as a result all share alike in the same material ridicule of the physical battle; of the "fight unspeakable" of which Raphael, with what sounds very much like unconscious irony — imposed on him, of course, by Milton — asks:

> . . . who, though with the tongue
> Of angels, can relate, or to what things
> Liken on earth conspicuous, that may lift
> Human imagination to such highth
> Of Godlike power . . .   (VI, 297—301)

Satan's invention of artillery leads to the farcical climax of the war as an image of the failure of moral understanding. It is the absolute expression of Satan's attempt to meet spiritual truth by material means. The "raping" of Heaven's "earth" for explosive material is a typical Satanic act, paralleling the later building of Pandemonium in Hell. Satan and his followers are anti-creative, perverting God's creation for infernal ends:

> . . . in a moment up they turned
> Wide the celestial soil, and saw beneath
> The originals of nature in their crude
> Conception; sulphurous and nitrous foam
> They found, they mingled, and with subtle art,
> Concocted and adusted they reduced
> To blackest grain . . .   (VI, 509—16)

And Raphael does not miss the opportunity to draw the parallel with man. "Yet haply of thy race" he tells Adam,

> In future days, if malice should abound,
> Some one intent on mischief, or inspired
> With devilish machination might devise
> Like instrument to plague the sons of men
> For sin, on war and mutual slaughter bent.   (VI, 502—6)

The battle formation which the rebel angels take around the artillery is itself an example of Satanic fraud, but it is also a potently ironic image which expresses the essential emptiness or "hollowness" of Satan's thought and action:

> Approaching gross and huge; in hollow cube
> Training his devilish enginry, impaled
> On every side with shadowing squadrons deep
> To hide the fraud . . .   (VI, 552—55)

The good angels suffer their greatest physical ridicule at the hands of Satan's artillery, and the image becomes so ludicrously comic that the reader feels almost guilty for laughing at the celestial warriors:

> . . . whom they hit, none on their feet might stand
> Though standing else as rocks, but down they fell
> By thousands, angel on archangel rolled,
> The sooner for their arms . . .   (VI, 592—95)

Their intended means of attack, their arms, become their downfall: "Unarmed, they might / Have easily as spirits, evaded swift / By quick contraction" (IV, 595—97). They are caught, as it were, in their own error. And insult is added most painfully to injury with the mockery poured on them by Satan and his cohorts, who satirize the position of the good angels by referring to their artillery in terms of rational argument:

> Leader, the terms we sent were terms of weight
> Of hard contents, and full of force urged home.   (VI, 621—22)

This satirical barb is more appropriate than intended by the speaker, for the whole spurious activity of warfare is in fact an extended metaphor for all pragmatic attempts to resolve the moral question, including that of imperfect discursive reasoning. And, too, the irony of the artillery episode is deepened if we remember an image of Satan's self-induced torment of mind from an earlier section of the narrative, a mind which

> . . . boils in his tumultuous breast
> And like a devilish engine back recoils
> Upon himself . . .   (IV, 16–18)

Michael's angels, having suffered ridicule as the outcome of Satan's invention of artillery, now blunder into even greater ridicule in the mountain throwing episode. In uprooting the trees of Heaven to use them as weapons the good angels continue Satan's gross error of trusting to material might and, indeed, carry it to sublime lengths. But the most damning aspect of their action is that it is a perversion of God's creation; they are helping do what Satan himself had threatened Abdiel he would do, "turn this heaven itself into the hell / Thou fablest" (VI, 291–92). And to add to this act of uncreation, there is an obvious parody of epic battle imagery which also serves to satirize the good angels, because like Satan's host they are operating within an epic battle mentality:

> From their foundations loosening to and fro,
> They plucked the seated hills, with all their load,
> Rocks, waters, woods, and, by the shaggy tops
> Up lifting, bore them in their hands . . .   (VI, 643–46)

Any doubts about Milton's detached and disapproving attitude towards this behaviour should be dispelled by the harsh irony – the words are Raphael's but the irony is Milton's – of the lines describing the angels' decision to use such extreme measures:

> Rage prompted them at length, and found them arms
> Against such hellish mischief fit to oppose.   (VI, 635–36)

The reader feels uneasy to see the good angels motivated by such a Satanic passion as rage; and the reason why the angels are now able to find such "fit" weapons to oppose the "hellish mischief" of Satan and his followers is that the relationship between the two sides has become for the time being purely quantative rather than qualitative, an opposition purely of physical against physical. The good angels have reduced themselves temporarily to their opponents' level by involving themselves with them in a common error; and the parenthetical comment – is it Raphael's or Milton's? – "(behold the excellence, the power, which God hath in his mighty angels placed!)" (VI, 637–38), is savagely ironic and sarcastic.

In the mutual hill-throwing episode – it is significant that both sides quickly get into the act – the war reaches its comical-farcical extreme, but the scene is ominous as well as comic in its chaos. The spurious reliance on external and material forces which the struggle has shown itself to be has achieved no positive result in terms of the real battle of good against evil. Satanic delusions have been in control and the only result has been to turn Heaven into discord, described in imagery readily recognized as belonging to Hell rather than to Heaven, and also paralleling the discord between Adam and Eve, and the world around them, following the fall:

> So hills amid the air encountered hills,
> Hurled to and fro with jaculation dire,
> That under ground they fought in dismal shade;
> Infernal noise; war seemed a civil game
> To this uproar; horrid confusion heaped
> Upon confusion rose: and now all heaven
> Had gone to wrack, with ruin overspread ...   (VI, 664–70)

And like the fall, the situation in Heaven arose from what was essentially a failure in faith, a failure in which the good angels are also temporarily involved, so that they are for the moment no better or worse than those they stand against, and therefore unable to dispose of them.

The war in Heaven has degenerated into a condition of stalemate and confusion. "Whence in perpetual fight" says God:

> ... they needs must last
> Endless, and no solution found.
> War wearied hath performed what war can do.   (VI, 693–95)

"War wearied hath performed what war can do." One is reminded of a similar passage from the end of *Samson Agonistes*:

> ... Samson hath quit himself
> Like Samson, and heroicly hath finished
> A life heroic ...   (*S.A.*, 1709–11)

Samson, by whose strength "with what trivial weapon came to hand / The jaw of a dead ass, his sword of bone, / A thousand foreskins fell" (*S.A.*, 142–44), is an almost purely heroic figure, performing and ending his mission by heroic, that is, physical, means, achieving all that he can by such means. The deeds of Christ, however, are "above heroic". Indeed the whole "argument" of *Paradise Lost* is "not less but more heroic than the wrath / Of stern Achilles" (IX, 14–15); its heroism is that of moral rather than physical strength and courage. And just as Samson's physical strength had accomplished all it was capable of, so the military angels have done all they can do, leaving the physical impasse of the war to be resolved in the only possible way, through the morally triumphant figure of Christ.

Christ's resolution of the state of discord by means of a personal triumph over evil parallels his future redemption of mankind as outlined by Michael in the last books of the poem. It is significant that Christ in triumph over Satan is creative in victory, contrasting with the negative battle waged by Michael's angels. He not only re-establishes creative order in Heaven by driving out the disruptive forces of Satan, but he also repairs the damage done to God's order by the good angels themselves:

At his command the uprooted hills retired
Each to his place, they heard his voice, and went
Obsequious, heaven his wonted face renewed,
And with fresh flowerets hill and valley smiled.   (VI, 781—84)

The misguided extremes of futile violence indulged in by both sides during
the war is also contrasted with the temperate virtue of Christ, who checks
his strength so as not to cause wild destruction:

Yet half his strength he put not forth, but checked
His thunder in mid-volley, for he meant
Not to destroy, but root them out of heaven.   (VI, 853—55)

None the less the difficulty remains that Christ's victory appears to be
one of physical strength:

He on his impious foes right onward drove,
Gloomy as night; under his burning wheels
The steadfast empyrean shook throughout,
All but the throne it self of God. Full soon
Among them he arrived; in his right hand
Grasping ten thousand thunders, which he sent
Before him . . .   (VI, 831—37)

But again it must be remembered that the perspective from which this is
seen is still the limited one of the immediate narrator, Raphael, and not
that of God or the divinely inspired poet. Indeed it is an important part of
the whole complex image of the war that the image of the victorious Christ
should be seen from the deluded perspective of the military angels. Both
Satan's forces and Michael's see Christ in their own image; not as he truly
is, a supreme moral force, but as a terrifying epic warrior triumphing as
they had sought to do, by sheer physical might. Raphael's memory of
Christ is of him as he

. . . as a herd
Of goats or timorous flock together thronged
Drove them before him thunderstruck, pursued
With terror and with furies to the bounds
And crystal wall of heaven . . .   (VI, 856—60)

But even this image of violence is exaggerated by the fallen angels themselves, thus emphasizing the uncertain credibility of their memories of
the event. Raphael sees them pursued only to the wall of Heaven, when
"headlong themselves they threw / Down from the verge of heaven" (VI,
864—65). But Moloch, speaking to the assembled multitude in Pandemonium, recalls being scourged and pursued by Christ throughout their
broken retreat to Hell:

When the fierce foe hung on our broken rear
Insulting, and pursued as through the deep,

With what compulsion and laborious flight
We sunk thus low? . . .   (II, 78–81)

The reason for Moloch's confusion of recall is a truth which he would never realize, that his image of a scourging Christ is no more than a rationalization of his own personal torment deriving from his rebellion against God.

Thus we see that the equivocal nature of the image of Christ in this section of the poem serves to betray the central truth about the military angels on both sides; namely that they are unable adequately to perceive that moral conflict is a matter of the individual's obedience to the moral law, and accordingly of the individual's faith. The false image of the victorious warrior Christ is a creation of their own, a crude rationalization of their own inability fully to understand the personal locus of faith and morality. The true image is that of the victory, based on faith, of the one over the many, the renewal of the personal element of morality which was originally established by Abdiel in his single opposition to Satan. The whole image of the war thus is one of a moving away from that genuine individual faith and moral heroism toward the spurious physical encounters of the war itself, then back again to a triumphant celebration of the personal moral victory. In this it is a statement of what was almost certainly Milton's own most deeply felt conviction.

On a superficial level the image of the war in Heaven is that of the triumph of good over evil. But this is not where its importance lies, either for Adam to whom the narrative is directly addressed, or for the meaning of the poem as a whole. Its importance is as an image of imperfect understanding and imperfect faith, and its lesson is one for the individual: that the defence against evil lies within, in the steadfastness of the individual faith and not in physical barriers against it, not in the strength of the big battalions with which to oppose it. And it is ironic that Adam should have been set to learn this lesson from Raphael, who himself betrayed his limited understanding of it. For when Adam eventually faces Satan he too is betrayed by the imperfection of his faith, though in his case the imperfection takes a different form.

And if it might seem difficult, finally, to accept that Raphael and the rest of the faithful angels should have been so inadequate in their understanding of the difference between physical and moral strength, then it should be remembered that Milton was not really concerned with the nature of angels but with that of man; and he would thus not perhaps have been to much concerned about misrepresenting the former if in the process he could say something about the latter. And that the account of the war in Heaven, seen as we have looked at it in this essay, does say something about man is, I think, clearly indicated by the history of his religious struggles through the centuries.

7

The Necessary Fall

As I write this I have beside me on the wall a reproduction from Massaggio's *Adamo-e-Eva Cacciati dal Paradiso* from the Chiesa del Carmine in Florence. A typical Renaissance illustration, it shows Adam and Eve emerging from the gate of Paradise while overhead hovers the figure of the Archangel Gabriel with his sword. Set against the closing lines of *Paradise Lost* it is puny, unimaginative, for here is one of the great images of the poem, tremendous in its scope and imaginative power:

>   ... from the other hill
> To their fixed station, all in bright array,
> The cherubim descended; on the ground
> Gliding meteorous, as evening mist
> Risen from a river o'er the marish glides,
> And gathers ground fast at the labourer's heel
> Homeward returning. High in front advanced,
> The brandished sword of God before them blazed,
> Fierce as a comet ...
>   ... whereat
> In either hand the hastening angel caught
> Our lingering parents, and to the eastern gate
> Led them direct, and down the cliff as fast
> To the subjected plain, then disappeared.
> They looking back, all the eastern side beheld
> Of Paradise, so late their happy seat,
> Waved over by that flaming brand, the gate
> With dreadful faces thronged and fiery arms:
> Some natural tears they dropped, but wiped them soon;
> The world was all before them, where to choose
> Their place of rest, and providence their guide.
> They hand in hand with wandering steps and slow,
> Through Eden took their solitary way.   (XII, 626—49)

Of all the problems posed by *Paradise Lost* the most important, the one to which all others must eventually be referred, is that of the fall itself. The poem seems to be quite clear on the matter: the fall resulted from disobedience and led to disaster:

> Of man's first disobedience, and the fruit
> Of that forbidden tree, whose mortal taste
> Brought death into the world, and all our woe.   (I, 1—3)

But faced with the magnificent complexity of the poem's closing lines, few readers will remain content with this as a complete and final summary of the nature and meaning of the fall. Though the poem begins as a "justification of the ways of God to men" we may be more inclined to leave it as giving a justification of humanity's ways to God.

Thus far in these essays we have been concerned primarily with events leading up to the fall. And we seem to have been led towards two apparently contradictory conclusions: first that man, having been created strong enough to stand, fell by his own choice, by the exercise of the free will given him by God; and second that none the less the fall seems to have been inevitable from the beginning, that when God says that man "will fall" He is simply recognizing this inevitability. Or is He? Is He perhaps stating what is His will, namely that man should fall. If we feel, as I think we do, that despite his alleged freedom man *is* fated to fall, then his fall must surely be the will of God. "... necessity and chance" God declares, "Approach not me, and what I will is fate" (VII, 172–73). The fall of man would seem to be something which did "approach" God and therefore not something to be left to necessity or chance. For instance, Milton is careful so to arrange matters in allowing Satan to find Eve alone as to ensure that this "fatal" meeting is not the result of "fate" or chance, but of man's deliberate choice. But if the fall is the will of God, then is it still possible to accept that man had free will and fell by his own free choice? Or that the fall was a disaster from which all man's subsequent troubles have stemmed? Like the fallen angels we seem to be in "wandering mazes lost" and perhaps should turn to look at the fall itself.

The immediate consequences of the fall, as it affects first Eve and then Adam, may strike the reader at least in the beginning as somewhat contradictory. For Eve the results are a rapid loss of judgement, she appears as if drunk, and an even more rapid moral deterioration as she first thinks of deceiving Adam for her own advantage and then grossly deceives herself as to her motives in sharing her discovery with him. But the effect on Adam seems quite different. For the first time, except perhaps when he speaks to Raphael about Eve's influence on him, he is likely to win the full sympathy of the reader; for the first time he speaks as a fully recognizable human being to whom the reader can relate. But to understand why this is so, we should go back to look at the "unfallen" Adam.

In his account of the creation of the world, Raphael tells Adam that God created man "self-knowing" (VII, 510); but ironically it is this very quality that the Son accuses Adam of lacking when he comes to the Garden to judge Adam and Eve after the fall (X, 144–56). "Hadst thou known thyself aright" he tells Adam, Eve would not have been able to sway him in the way she did. And although in discussion with Raphael before the fall of Eve's influence on himself, the limitations of Adam's judgement may clearly be seen to stem from this influence, there are other less obvious but persistent indications of such limitations through-out the account of life in the Garden. Before the fall all Adam's speeches are prefaced with some kind of title, or almost stage direction. "To whom our general ancestor replied . . . " (IV, 659); openings such as this reflect how Adam perceives himself, not in his individuality and personality but in his "role". And the same is true of Eve, too, though she is more inclined to "break out" of her role; and of Adam in his words addressed to her. He speaks to her not as a woman or a wife, but in her role as "daughter of God and man" (IV, 660), for instance, and he seems always to speak in the tones of general authority; never for himself personally but for his position. He has an understanding of his role as father of his race, of his role as "our general ancestor"; he has an understanding of his own impor-tance, but no understanding of his humanity, of his "frailty". Believing himself to be "godlike", flattered by his dominance over all the beasts of his world, Adam remains ignorant of this too human quality.

This perhaps is not altogether true. Like Eve, but to a much lesser extent, Adam does occasionally show an understanding of his human frailty. As when, for instance, he agrees with Raphael's admonishment to be "lowly wise; / Think only what concerns thee and thy being", but then adds somewhat wistfully,

> But apt the mind or fancy is to rove
> Unchecked, and of her roving is no end.   (VIII, 188–89)

Only to return once more to "correctness" with:

> . . . but to know
> That which before us lies in daily life,
> Is the prime wisdom . . .   (VIII, 192–94)

Though he speaks to God of his essential imperfection when seeking the creation of Eve, his awareness of this imperfection is intuitive. He is not sufficiently aware of its nature to know that what he needs to overcome it is also what can destroy him. But though he goes on to reveal to Raphael just how limited his awareness is, to reveal indeed the same lack of under-standing of his own nature and Eve's as the Son was later to charge him with, he does give us a glimpse of a greater humanity, particularly as he defends himself against Raphael's charge of being "transported" by an "outside", of being carried away by Eve's physical beauty. Not her "out-side formed so fair" he says,

> So much delights me as those graceful acts,
> Those thousand decencies that daily flow
> From all her words and actions . . .   (VIII, 600–602)

Though Adam has some awareness of the nature of evil – as he shows, for instance, in his reaction to Eve's dream – and of the need for vigilance against it, he is unaware of just how close the tree of the knowledge of

good and evil stands to the tree of life. He does not really understand the
danger. In response to Raphael's injunction as to the need for obedience,
he exclaims:

> *. . . If ye be found*
> *Obedient?* Can we want obedience then
> To him, or possibly his love desert
> Who formed us from the dust . . .   (V, 513–16)

And during the account of the war in Heaven he is amazed that war could
be so "near the peace of God in bliss" (VII, 55). In the scene immediately
preceding the fall, though he expresses a fear for Eve's safety " . . . lest
harm / Befall thee severed from me" (IX, 251–52), and though he realizes
that Satan watches

> . . . with greedy hope to find
> His wish and best advantage, us asunder,
> Hopeless to circumvent us joined, where each
> To other speedy aid might lend at need.   (IX, 257–60)

yet despite all these words he lets Eve go, on the formal ground that to
prevent her would be to limit her freedom. This is all right for God, and
for Adam in his role as "God" for Eve. But it shows his failure to understand the nature of his human bond with her, shows that he is not really
any more aware of her human frailty than he is of his own. And when she
returns with the apple he is amazed that she could have fallen:

> How art thou lost, how on a sudden lost,
> Defaced, deflowered, and now to death devote?   (IX, 900–901)

The actuality of her weakness, of her humanity, is totally beyond his
comprehension. He cannot believe that one so beautiful and complete, so
perfect in his eyes, could have fallen so fast, so low. As Eve is "credulous"
(IX, 644), so is Adam.

With the fall Adam is suddenly confronted with a real test of his
obedience to God, one that is no longer formal, in which words are no
longer enough. He must act. But though Eve may have shown herself to be
indeed "wanton", she cannot be "lopped" like the wanton growth of the
flowery arbours. This is his Eve, part of himself; he begins to see more
clearly what he had understood only intuitively when he sought her
creation. For the first time we see Adam completely forsake the formality
of his role and speak not from an importance and wisdom of position, but
from the very heart of his *human* being, from personal feeling and personal
fear:

> And me with thee hath ruined, for with thee
> Certain my resolution is to die;
> How can I live without thee, how forgo
> Thy sweet converse and love so dearly joined,
> To live again in these wild woods forlorn?   (IX, 906–10)

There is nothing formal in Adam's sudden imaginative ability to see that to live in the Garden without Eve is to live in "these wild woods / Forlorn". A paradise without Eve is for him already a paradise lost. So he makes his choice, between his responsibility to God, to his creator, and his responsibility to himself, to his own humanity. And though, as we have seen, to God the cause of the fall may be Adam's failure "to know himself aright", what strikes the reader more forcibly is that in its outcome it may rather be seen as a first step toward that self-understanding.

The process, however, is not a straightforward one. Ironically, at the moment when he begins to understand the true nature of his link with Eve, Adam fails to realize that in its existing form the link is already broken:

> So forcible within my heart I feel
> The bond of nature draw me to my own,
> My own in thee, for what thou art is mine;
> Our state cannot be severed, we are one,
> One flesh; to lose thee were to lose my self.   (IX, 955–59)

But the bond is already severed. The symbolic parting of hands when Eve left him before the fall has become a reality, witnessed by Eve's thoughts after eating the apple. The Eve who would take Adam to death with her rather than face the prospect of being replaced by "another Eve" and then at once convince herself that "Adam shall share with me in bliss or woe: / So dear I love him" (IX, 831–32) is not the Eve with whom Adam thinks of himself "by love so dearly joined". And there is a suggestion of selfishness in Adam's response too. Though his first thought is of Eve, "How art thou lost . . . ", it is of himself he mainly thinks, of what is to happen to him if Eve is no more: "How shall I live without thee . . . To lose thee were to lose my self". Adam is not suddenly transformed from the perfect innocent to the perfect human being. Rather he simply becomes more human, with all the frailty of humanity, with the beginnings of a more adequate understanding of what it is to be "frail man".

Adam does not realize, as I have said, that the bond between himself and Eve has been broken and must be forged anew before they will be ready to leave the Garden once more hand in hand. At first both he and Eve "feel / Divinity within them breeding wings / Wherewith to scorn the earth" (IX, 1009–11). But their love-making lacks the ceremony, the harmonious beauty of their pre-fallen state, as Adam

> . . . forbore not glance or toy
> Of amorous intent, well understood
> Of Eve, whose eye darted contagious fire.
> Her hand he seized, and to a shady bank,
> Thick overhead with verdant roof embowered
> He led her nothing loath . . .   (IX, 1034–39)

It is no orgy, the adjustment of tone is nice; but unfallen Adam would never have "seized" Eve by the hand; and now their love-making leads only to feelings of guilt and shame. Adam must indeed sink into abysmal depths of bitterness and self-reproach before he is able to come out of the darkness into the light of true humanity.

We have seen elsewhere how it is Eve's role eventually to lead the way towards redemption. But even before this Adam in his bitterest moments shows signs of his new humanity. He tries, for instance, to anticipate Eve by taking the blame and consequences of the fall on himself, but his thoughts are only too humanly mixed:

> . . . But from me what can proceed
> But all corrupt . . .
> On me, me only, as the source and spring
> Of all corruption, all the blame lights due.
> So might the wrath. Fond wish! Couldst thou support
> That burden, heavier than the earth to bear
> Than all the world much heavier, though divided
> With that bad Woman?   (X, 824—37)

When "that bad woman" is sufficiently tactless to intrude by her mere presence on his bitter thoughts, even his "Out of my sight, thou serpent" (X, 867) is in a way an improvement on the earlier formality of his address to her. And in response to the simplicity of her "Forsake me not thus, Adam" (X, 914) we hear him for the first time, and indeed from now on (X, 1013; XI, 141; XI, 226), address her not as "mother of mankind" or "daughter of God", but directly and personally, simply as Eve. Just as the earlier forms of address had served to accentuate the formal nature of their respective roles and of the bond between them, "He for God only, she for God in him", so this change seems to symbolize a new awareness of their joint humanity and their separate personality. And with this awareness, and the unselfish concern for each other that accompanies it, comes a renewed ability to speak to God, a beginning at least of the end of their alienation from Him.

The wedding bower of Adam and Eve lies, as we have seen, at the centre of *Paradise Lost*, and the wedding bond — formed at their creation, broken at the fall and resealed as a sign of hope at the close — forms the central symbol of its image of the human condition. In the poem we see Adam and Eve move through innocence, fall and repentence, to a point at which they are at least in the way of achieving a real understanding of love, a love that binds them to one another, to their humanity and to God. The Garden is a beautiful image of that love. It is not a garden of "nice art / In beds and curious knots, but nature boon / Poured forth profuse . . . " (IV, 241—43). It is allowed to grow in beautiful wilderness; yet it is not allowed to grow "untended". Eve reflects this beautiful wilderness: her "unadorned tresses" are worn "Dishevelled, but in wanton

ringlets waved / As the vine curls her tendrils, which implied / Subjection"
(IV, 304—308). Her wanton ringlets are not only symbolic of her innocent
role as woman, implying a loving subjection to Adam, but also of her fall
into self-subjection. Her natural inclination to "wantonness" remains
innocent while tended by Adam's love, while they walk hand in hand;
but when she withdraws her hand from his, when she rejects the limits
love places on her freedom, then wantonness falls into depravity and the
enthralment of a selfish, ungoverned passion. Though, like the Garden,
it is not subjected to the tortuous rigours of "curious knots", Eve's freedom lies within the bonds of tender care, of love.

And as Eve must learn that obedience in love is not thraldom, but a
necessary, desirable and indeed natural outcome of that love, so Adam
must learn that obedience in love is not a "nice art". In his original state
of innocence Adam mouths the words of loving obedience to God: as
"God hath set / Labour and rest, as day and night to men / Successive . . ."
so men must seek repose (IV, 612—14), as God requires order and obedience in all things, they must rise early to "reform / Yon flowery arbours"
and "lop their wanton growth". But where in all his correctness is Adam's
spontaneity? Where is the loving attitude we see in Eve as she goes forth

> . . . among her fruits and flowers,
> To visit how they prospered, bud and bloom,
> Her nursery; they at her coming sprung,
> And touched by her fair tendance gladlier grew?   (VIII, 44—47)

Adam's obedience and his love for God seem mechanical. As Eve's love
may lack something of the necessary and natural bond of obedience,
Adam's obedience lacks the necessary freedom of "fair tendance". Both
must come to learn more fully the nature of love, whether it be love for
each other or for God; that is, selfless love, given willingly, which entails
not mindless subjection but a great freedom. The Son reproves Adam
after the fall with the words "adorned / She was indeed, and lovely to
attract / Thy love, not thy subjection . . . " (X, 151—53). And even
Satan's words when he first sees Adam and Eve and speaks of them as
"Imparadised in one another's arms" (IV, 506), full of envy as his words
are, they may still have an undertone, through the similarity of sound, of
"imprisoned", just as Satan himself before his fall felt imprisoned by
God's love. It is not until after the fall that Adam and Eve come to realize
a love free of this element of subjection, a love reflected in Eve's
expression of her readiness to move beyond the insular wall of an innocent
paradise into a world "obscure / And wild" (XI, 283—84). To Adam
she says:

> . . . but now lead on;
> In me is no delay; with thee to go
> Is to stay here; without thee here to stay

Is to go hence unwilling; thou to me
Art all things under heaven . . .   (XII, 614–18)

How far Eve has come from the self-pride and vanity of her creation, when like Narcissus she fell in love with her own image; from the wilful independence of her final parting from Adam before the fall! No longer does she perceive herself as " . . . Eve with perfect beauty adorned" (IV, 634); no longer does personal vanity obscure her love for Adam. She has come to recognize that the world was not created, as she had thought, for her eyes alone (IV, 657–58); that she is not a "Goddess humane" (IX, 732), but simply Eve. Though she laments the loss of Paradise she comes to recognize, as does Adam, the paradise that lies within a selfless love, freely given.

The whole process of Adam's, and Eve's, fall and ultimate hope of redemption is a learning process, a learning process as much concerned with the love of God as with the love of each other. Before the fall Raphael counsels Adam concerning the love due to God:

My self and all the angelic host that stand
In sight of God enthroned, our happy state
Hold, as you yours, while our obedience holds;
On other surety none; freely we serve,
Because we freely love, as in our will
To love or not; in this we stand or fall.   (V, 535–40)

If Adam understood the necessary conjunction of freedom, obedience and love he did so only intuitively; and although we hear God claim that "Happier, had it sufficed him to have known / Good by it self and evil not at all" (XI, 88–89), this is not the sentiment expressed by the totality of the poem. There the greater value is placed on a love not only freely given but consciously willed; willed with a full understanding of the nature of that love, the kind of love that comes after the fall rather than before it. Against the words of God just quoted we must listen to those of the Son after Adam and Eve have again been able to speak to God:

See Father, what first-fruits on earth are sprung
From thy implanted grace in man . . .
Fruits of more pleasing savour, from thy seed
Sown with contrition in his heart, than those
Which his own hand manuring all the trees
Of Paradise could have produced, ere fallen
From innocence . . .   (XI, 22–30)

God has harvested the fruits of love freely given in a full and "knowledge-able" understanding of its implications, fruits of more pleasing savour to God than any that have been produced by the state of innocence. These fruits are "sprung / From thy implanted grace in man"; but we have seen that this grace was only available after Adam and Eve had actively willed

their own redemption. Before the fall, but of course with full foreknowledge of it, God had said that "Man shall not quite be lost, but saved who
will, / Yet not of will in him, but grace in me" (III, 173—74); and here the
form of the statement is such as to put the maximum emphasis on the
need for a positive act of will.

Grace is essential, but the will must first be present. Then, says God
" . . . once more I will renew / His lapsed powers . . . that he may know
how frail / His fallen condition is . . . " (III, 175—80). Redemption for
Adam is a learning process, a process of increasing knowledge of himself;
at least a rebuilding of the intuitive knowledge of good lost at the fall,
at most the attainment of a higher, more complex kind of knowledge. The
learning process is continued throughout Michael's narrative of historic
events to come, as Adam is called on to learn from what he sees and hears,
often indeed by his mistakes. As when, for instance, he mistakes the vision
of the "bevy of fair women" as one of nature "fulfilled in all her ends",
only to be told that "Those tents thou saw'st so pleasant, were the tents /
Of wickedness . . . " (XI, 602—608). And almost the final words of
Michael seem surely to express explicitly the implicit theme of *Paradise
Lost* in summing up what Adam has learned:

```
. . . only add
Deeds to thy knowledge answerable . . .
. . . then wilt thou not be loath
To leave this Paradise, but shalt possess
A paradise within thee, happier far.        (XII, 581—87)
```

This new Paradise, "happier far" than the one that has been lost, is to
derive from the exercise of free will "answerable" not to the innocent,
intuitive goodness of the Garden, but to knowledge, to understanding
granted perhaps by grace but not until the right to it has been hard won by
experience. Again we are reminded of Milton's words from *Areopagitica.*
Seen from this perspective, the fall of man becomes not so much a fall
as a natural and necessary movement toward a fully realized human state.
Though He created man with free will, God knew that despite this —
rather indeed because of it — man would fall. Satan was instrumental to
His designs, as he was indeed to be later, for instance, in the trials of Jonah
and, of course, in the temptation of Christ himself. Though the "pendant
world" would seem to hang in a balance between God and Satan, between
obedience and disobedience, between slavery and freedom, between
jealous, destructive hate and creative, life-giving love, it is none the less
forever linked by its "golden chain" to Heaven, not to Hell. Just as God
"allowed" the war in Heaven to reveal the imperfect understanding by
both the loyal and rebel angels of the nature of goodness, so for His own
purposes He allows the contest between Satan and man. God is
omnipotent, and in opposing Him Satan cannot be other than self-deluded.

Though "vaunting aloud" he is "racked with deep despair". He is a glorious and daunting foe, and could be no less if man is to fall by his guile; but by comparison with God he is darkness to His light. It is not just Satan's words but his self that has "Semblance of worth, not substance" (I, 529). His "legions" are "abject and lost" (I, 312), like autumn leaves scattered in the wind (I, 301–303), and the great Archangel himself, the great heroic pretender to God's throne, is depicted as an old man leaning on his spear like a walking stick "to support uneasy steps" (I, 295), " . . . such resting found the sole / Of unblessed feet" (I, 237–38). This incipiently comic image of Satan is no match for the image of God "High throned above all highth", bending down his eye to view his works (III, 56–59). Right from the beginning we are left in no doubt as to the final outcome of their "battle":

> So stretched out huge in length the arch-fiend lay,
> Chained on the burning lake, nor ever thence
> Had risen, or heaved his head, but that the will
> And high permission of all-ruling heaven
> Left him at large to his own dark designs,

that he might see, and that we might see

> How all his malice served but to bring forth
> Infinite goodness, grace, and mercy shown
> On man by him seduced, but on himself
> Treble confusion, wrath and vengeance poured.   (I, 209–20)

If we believe this, if we believe that God is omnipotent and all-seeing, that He is goodness and light, one who brings forth goodness even out of evil, then with the evidence of the whole poem before us we must believe that God foresaw the fall as a means of furthering man's understanding of his own nature and role.

This does not mean that the fall is any less a tragedy, a point I shall be discussing in a later essay. It does not mean that the fall did not bring "death into the world, and all our woe". Nor does it mean that God's foreknowledge caused Adam's fall; man was indeed made sufficient to have stood, had he willed to do so. But it does mean that God set the pledge of obedience and faith knowing that man would break that pledge; knowing indeed that man must break the pledge and face the consequences if he was to realize a true and full understanding of his humanity, if he was ultimately to make the choice freely and knowingly to stand with God.

This view of *Paradise Lost* may serve to resolve some at least of its apparent contradictions. It also sustains it as a justification of the ways of God to men. But it may do more than this. Paradoxically it may also enable us to read *Paradise Lost* as an image of the human condition essentially humanist in spirit, even to the extent almost of dispensing with the specifically Christian element as no more than a necessary superstructure. Though I would hasten to add that I am not claiming that it is *necessary* for us to see it in this way; and from the point of view of the origins of the poem in Milton's intentions such a view of it belongs certainly to the subconscious levels of the complex of experience and belief expressed in the poem.

What I am suggesting is that the picture of Adam and Eve leaving the Garden to face the world, the world with all its terrors and hardships and they with all their own weakness and frailty, is the poem's ultimate image of the triumph of the individual human spirit, of the poet's humanist belief in man. Against the world ahead of them, of which Michael has in vision and story given Adam such a harrowing and terrifying picture, is set the beauty, the harmony, the absolute peace of the Garden they are leaving behind. They go forth "sorrowing" as God has said they should, "yet in peace". Peace based on the hope that despite the odds man will eventually triumph, not from an arbitrary obedience to any absolute belief, not from an unquestioning conformity to any all embracing creed or system, comfortable, attractive, secure, even beautiful as a life of such conformity might seem to be; but through a belief in himself based on a fully knowledgeable understanding of his own nature.

The state of innocence, like the ideal state of childhood, is a necessary stage in human development, one to be left behind with intense regret perhaps, and looked back on with nostalgia and with pity for what is lost by its passing. But left behind it must be if man is to achieve his full adult stature, is to realize the ideal of his humanity. Whether this realization is put to the service of humanism or religion is immaterial, for it is essential to both. Neither man's regard for God nor his own self-regard can be based on anything short of full self-understanding. When Milton in *Paradise Regained* turned to the religious working out of this image in the person of Christ he did so, as we shall see in another essay, at the expense of man's humanity; but this does not negate the validity of the image.

We might return, by way of conclusion, to the image with which the poem itself ends, that of Adam and Eve leaving the Garden. The poem's epic space has now contracted from its original immensity to the solitary walk from Paradise, but there is promise of new space ahead; the "world was all before them". We have already seen how the inward movement in space of the poem parallels an increasing inwardness of its psychological action; and this final image points to the development of a new epic spirit, towards which the descent from Paradise, the "fall", provides the impetus. From being simply part of the whole cosmos of the poem, Adam and Eve have moved first inward toward a concentration on self that has alienated them from their environment. They are now again ready to move outward, but in a new, more dynamic relationship to their own selves, to each other and to their world. The development is clearest with Eve. Her inward movement into self follows the inward movement of the poem and culminates in the complete selfishness of her response immediately after eating the apple; and then, as part of the corresponding outward movement, the development of Eve's psyche also turns outward. Unlike Satan (and also, for that matter, Adam until rescued by Eve), who continues to be more and more lost in the maze of self which for him is Hell, Eve turns outward towards selflessness, but on a new basis of self-knowledge and self-discovery. Against this image, the alternative of remaining within the Garden suggests a fate worse than the death which they now must ultimately face: a lack of self-discovery, of expansiveness, a form indeed of nothingness. They are now become the "true wayfaring Christians" of whom Milton writes in *Areopagitica*.

8

Patterns of Tragedy

The sturdy soul of the tragic author seizes upon suffering and uses it only as a means by which joy may be wrung out of existence, but it is not to be forgotten that he is enabled to do so only because of his belief in the greatness of human nature and because, though he has lost the child's faith in life, he has not lost his far more important faith in human nature. A tragic writer does not have to believe in God, but he must believe in man.[1]

The author of these lines believes that tragedy cannot be written in the modern age because the essential belief in man has been lost, and consequently there can be no stories except those which make the age "still more aware of its trivial miseries". If this is true − or in so far as it is true − and, if I am right in arguing that *Paradise Lost* is as much an affirmation of man as of God, then it may help to suggest why the poem has a special attraction for the modern reader and also serve to emphasize its tragic element as the basis of that attraction. For, as the author of the words quoted above goes on to say, "our need for the consolation of tragedy has not passed with the passing of our ability to conceive it", and it is in poetry that we look for that consolation. Poetry, he says quoting Santayana, "is religion which is no longer believed", but it has the power "to revive in us a sort of temporary or provisional credence, and the nearer it can come to producing an illusion of belief the greater its power as poetry". *Paradise Lost* I would suggest is pre-eminently a source of this power.

Paradise Lost is, of course, an epic and not a tragedy. But we know that many years before he wrote *Paradise Lost* Milton was thinking of a work in dramatic form, very likely a tragedy in the classical style of *Samson Agonistes*, to go under the title of *Adam Unparadised,* on the theme of the Genesis story. The great soliloquy of Satan at the beginning of Book IV of *Paradise Lost* is in fact thought to have been written originally as the opening speech of the projected drama. Why Milton did not go ahead with his tragedy we do not know, but that he still regarded the fall of man as in some way a tragedy is indicated by the opening lines of Book IX, the climactic book of the poem:

1. Joseph Wood Krutch, *The Modern Temper* (1929); quoted from Morris Weitz (ed.), *Problems in Aesthetics* (1970), p. 735.

> . . . I now must change
> These notes to tragic . . .   (IX, 5–6)

In what sense is the fall of man as it is portrayed in *Paradise Lost* a tragedy?

The description of the fall and its immediate consequences that follows on from the lines quoted above does not necessarily point to tragedy:

> . . . foul distrust, and breach
> Disloyal on the part of man, revolt
> And disobedience; on the part of heaven
> Now alienated, distance and distaste,
> Anger and just rebuke, and judgement given
> That brought into this world a world of woe,
> Sin and her shadow Death, and Misery,
> Death's harbinger . . .   (IX, 6–13)

This is not, at least on its own, the stuff of which tragedy is made. Nor do such statements as that of the narrator of the poem that man being "manifold in sin, deserved to fall" (X, 16) point to tragedy. The downfall of the thoroughly worthless or villainous person is not tragic, and the more completely and simply it is true that man "deserved to fall" the less tragic his fall is likely to seem. And, indeed, Milton goes on at the beginning of Book IX to claim his work not as a tragedy but as heroic poetry, as "argument / Not less but more heroic than the wrath / Of stern Archilles" (IX, 13–15). We must look then to the wider development of the story to discover the nature and pattern of it as tragedy.

Tragedy, if it is to arouse the pity and fear described first by Aristotle, or if it is to "seize upon suffering and use it as a means whereby joy may be wrung out of existence", cannot confine itself to the petty or commonplace in either the characters or the action. It must in some way be lifted above the common and ordinary. Adam and Eve as they first appear before us in noble guise are fully adequate to their tragic role:

> Two of far nobler shape, erect and tall,
> Godlike erect, with native honour clad
> In naked majesty, seemed lords of all,
> And worthy seemed, for in their looks divine
> The image of their glorious maker shone.   (IV, 288–92)

And the whole narrative leading up to the fall is full of great events. There is, indeed, no doubt that Milton's story of Adam and Eve provides a basis for tragedy; which still, however, requires development for it to take on tragic form. Or rather, as tragedy has not been seen as confined to a single form, the way in which the story is developed will determine which, if any, tragic pattern it assumes.

This is not the place for a detailed discussion of the nature of tragedy, but a brief outline may serve as a useful starting point for a consideration of the structure of tragedy in *Paradise Lost.* Tragedy is either the tragedy of circumstance or the tragedy of character, or a combination of the two. That is, the tragic hero is laid low by forces either external to himself or within himself, or by external forces combining with those within. A further distinction may be made in the case of external forces between those which are purely fortuitous, a matter of chance or of a purely capricious fortune, and those which are the result of some directing force, such as that of the gods in much Greek drama; and, in the case of tragedy resulting from inner forces, between that in which those forces are simple errors of judgement with no moral significance, and that in which moral weakness of some kind is specifically the cause of the tragedy. There are thus a number of possibilities, any of which may combine to form a large variety of possible tragic patterns, the common element in which is a central character of potentially tragic stature involved in events of potentially tragic proportions.

The earliest Greek tragedy was of the simplest sort; that is, tragedy brought about by wholly fortuitous external events, where the tragic hero could not be described as anything other than unfortunate. Later these events began to be imputed to the gods, but even here their influence remains largely capricious. As Gloucester has it in Shakespeare's *King Lear*:

> As flies to wanton boys, are we to th' Gods;
> They kill us for their sport.   (IV, i, 36–37)

Later still, with Aristotle, the element of character is emphasized, the so-called "tragic flaw"; but though there remains some doubt among commentators as to the meaning of some of his terms, this tragic flaw apparently does not necessarily involve suggestions of specifically moral weakness. For Aristotle tragedy is the paradox of the superior, noble hero who is none the less brought down by an error or weakness of judgement. Whether or not Aristotle himself meant this weakness to be understood as being of a moral kind, an increasingly didactic attitude to literature, particularly in the Roman era, led to the emphasis being placed more and more on moral weakness as the flaw in an otherwise perfect character.

The medieval world saw a return to a simpler pattern of external tragedy; but here, under the influence of Christianity, the notions of a purely capricious fortune, or of gods sporting thoughtlessly with the affairs of men, are replaced by the concept of God's providence as a force directing the apparently tragic events towards a good end. Tragedy is still moral, but as part of a moral scheme larger than a narrow didacticism based on individual weakness. Shakespeare's *Romeo and Juliet* may in a sense be seen as tragedy of this kind, in which the apparently "star-crossed" lovers by their deaths bring about the reconciliation of their feuding families and restore order to Verona. But Elizabethan, and particularly Shakespearian tragedy generally returns to the concept of the tragic flaw, usually with some implication of moral weakness. For Shakespeare, however, the purpose of tragedy is not didactic, or at least not immediately so; his interest is rather in the character of the tragic hero, in the psychological exploration of human strengths and weaknesses. External forces of a varying degree of importance are, of course, still present, but mostly they do little more than provide a framework within which the inner conflict is allowed to develop.

These then were some of the recognized and established patterns of tragedy available to Milton for imitation when he came to write *Paradise Lost* and to develop the tragic potentialities of its story. Some of the forms may be dismissed at once as being impossible to apply to the poem. God's reiterated insistence throughout the poem on man's free will, on man's own responsibility for his fall, if it is taken at its face value, would seem to exclude any pattern of tragedy depending solely on external forces, whether capricious or working towards some end. God's insistence, too, that though he foreknows the fall such foreknowledge "had no influence on their fault, / Which had no less proved certain unforeknown" (III, 118–19), would rule out any simple operation of providence as the basis of the tragedy. The opposite extreme, the tragedy purely of character, in which external forces play a wholly incidental role, presents a more difficult model. On the face of it, Satan's role in the fall is that of an external force that cannot be dismissed as irrelevent or incidental, but then the nature of that role itself needs further examination.

The Genesis story by itself provided at most the basis for tragedy on the Aristotelian model of an error of judgement on the part of an otherwise perfect hero. In the original simplicity of the story, Adam and Eve are seen as created in the image of God and any moral weakness imputed to them is the result rather than the cause of the fall. The fall under these circumstances could be the result of nothing other than an error of judgement, a failure to recognize what should be done, resulting from rational rather than moral weakness; though even then one might be inclined to worry about the source of the weakness in rationality. It is simply a paradox, the apparently perfect individual in circumstances of the utmost importance and for some inexplicable reason making the wrong choice. As the story is developed in the poem, however, we have ample evidence of what might be seen as moral weakness in both Adam and Eve before the fall; Eve's self-pride, Adam's uxoriousness, to give them their usual convenient labels. There is ample evidence for us to see this weakness as the immediate cause of their fall when it combines with the influence of an external force, that is Satan in the case of Eve, and Eve herself in the case of Adam. The pattern of tragedy is then the standard Elizabethan one of a fatal combination of character and circumstance, of moral weakness and external influence. Adam and Eve are placed in a situation with which their inner weakness renders them unable to cope; in other circumstances, or without their particular flaw they might have survived. These factors, together with their original nobility and the great significance for humanity of the events in which they are involved assure their tragic status.

This pattern, however, is dependent on a relatively straightforward, possibly simplistic, reading of the poem, paying heed as an explanation of the fall only to the suggestions of at least a potentiality for moral weakness in both Adam and Eve: in such episodes as Eve's dream or her initial response to her own beauty, and Adam's account to Raphael of the effect that Eve has on him. But a more subtle response to the poem such as has been suggested in some of the previous essays may have the effect of changing the tragic pattern; in fact of simplifying it by the elimination of some of its elements. Firstly, there is the position of Eve. We have discussed in the essay devoted to her role in the poem how Adam sees her as being needed in order to complete, to perfect himself; how his "masculine" quality of reason is supplemented by her "feminine" quality of sensibility, of creative imagination; how without him she is lacking support while without her he is barren; how in an all pervasive way the central image of the joining of hands has much more than its superficial meaning, giving to Adam's cry at the fall its true significance:

    . . . no, no, I feel
    The link of nature draw me . . .
    So forcible within my heart I feel
    The bond of nature draw me to my own,
    My own in thee, for what thou art is mine;
    Our state cannot be severed, we are one.
    One flesh; to lose thee were to lose myself.   (IX, 913–14 & 955–59)

Seen in this way Eve no longer stands outside Adam, between him and Satan. Rather she is within him, part of himself, the fatal flaw in his nature that makes him susceptible to Satan's wiles; though as we have seen she is also the means by which his redemption is made possible. Thus the dual tragedy of at first Eve and then of Adam is simplified into the single tragedy of man; though the pattern of an inner weakness, Eve, and an external force, Satan, remains.

The second simplification of the pattern depends on a recognition of the increasingly inward movement of the poem's action, from its beginnings at the outer edges of its infinitely large cosmos to its climax at the very centre, within the mind of man. Milton's materials for his poem, the Genesis story and the Christian tradition developed from it, had put the emphasis in the fall story on the role of Satan as tempter; and superficially this is also true of the poem. God, for instance, differentiates between Satan, who was "self-tempted" and therefore will not "find grace", and man, who was "deceived / By the other first" and therefore will do so

(III, 129—31). We have seen, however, how at any level of reading more subtle than the most superficial this distinction will not hold; how Adam and Eve, as much as Satan, act in response to forces within themselves. And the whole imaginative force of the poem is in this direction; towards, indeed, the possible ultimate elimination of the figure of Satan as anything more than the outward symbol of forces operating within the mind of man; towards seeing man as himself "self-tempted, self-depraved" by forces which are part of his own human nature. On this level of interpretation *Paradise Lost* becomes essentially a tragedy of character, in which external events are no more than a framework, and in which the paradox noted earlier as inherent in the original story is eliminated.

Earlier I suggested that, because of the emphasis on man's free will and God's insistence that his own foreknowledge played no part in the fall, a medieval type tragedy in which events are directed by the force of God's providence did not seem to be applicable. However, in our discussion of the fall it was found that the concept of the fall as part of God's providence could be reconciled with that of unfallen man's essential freedom. Though the fall remains a tragedy — just as, for instance, the deaths of Romeo and Juliet remain tragic even though we may see them as part of a tragedy of providence in which the disorders of Verona are resolved — though the fall remains a tragedy, both for what was lost by it and for much of its consequences for mankind, it none the less gave promise eventually of a greater good than any that had been destroyed by it. And, furthermore, not only was this inevitable process of good out of evil part of the divine plan, but also the fall itself was within that plan. God, having created man with a freedom that would allow him either to stand or to fall, knew none the less that he would fall; indeed that he must fall if he was to realize the full potential of his humanity. This view of the fall makes for a complex tragic pattern. It retains the element of the tragic flaw, the inner weakness, the emphasis on character, but makes this in itself part of the overriding divine plan.

The moral emphasis which came to be associated with the concept of the tragic flaw caused the tragic conflict to be viewed in one way or another as a conflict between good and evil, between right and wrong; the essentially "good" hero is led by his particular inner weakness in a more or less "wrong" direction. And as regards *Paradise Lost*, the tradition on which it was based saw the fall as a straightforward victory, even if only a temporary one, for evil over good. The poem itself tends to refine this conflict into one between what Adam knew to be his duty to God and what he felt to be his duty to himself, to his own human nature; and its status as a Christian epic makes it inevitable that this choice should ostensibly be weighted towards Adam's duty to God, that it should continue to be seen as a conflict between good and evil. But there is much in the poem, as we have seen in the course of these essays, which militates against such a straightforward view; which causes at least the twentieth-century reader to feel that Adam was at best placed in an impossible position, one in which either choice he made would be wrong. For Adam to have rejected Eve, he is likely to feel, would have been just as wrong, just as false, as to reject God. The conflict in this view is thus not one between good and evil but between two conflicting "goods"; which leads us to consider a further concept of tragedy, that associated with the name of the German philosopher, Hegel.

This theory, at least in the form in which I shall be considering it, should perhaps more properly be termed the Hegel–Bradley theory, since it represents Hegel's ideas as worked out and presented by the English literary critic A. C. Bradley, in his "Hegel's Theory of Tragedy" (*Oxford Lectures on Poetry*, 1923, pp. 69–95). Bradley is primarily working on material contained in Hegel's *Aesthetics*, but because of the form of this latter work (it was written up after Hegel's death from his lecture notes) there remains a good deal of controversy as to what he actually meant, and consequently some doubt among scholars as to whether or not in all respects Bradley's exposition accurately reproduces Hegel's ideas. This, however, is immaterial for the present purpose, since it is the theory itself and not the question as to whose ideas it represents that concerns us here. As a matter of convenience I shall continue to refer to it as Hegel's theory, but the reservations suggested should be kept in mind. Hegel's theory, then, is of interest to a study of *Paradise Lost* in that it allows, indeed requires, that the feelings, the act of will, which prompted Adam's action in deciding to follow Eve in eating the apple, and the forces in human nature from which these feelings derived, should be seen as good in themselves, evil as the consequences of their operation in this particular instance may have been. That is, that Adam's feelings for Eve at the moment of the fall need not be seen as necessarily evil and thus need not contradict our own instinctive response to it.

Hegel's theory of tragedy postulates an "ethical substance", being the sum total of powers that together "rule the world of man's will and action". These powers, divine in nature but expressed through the action of the individual human will, emerge in tragedy when there is a "conflict of spirit", a conflict between two or more of these powers operating separately, when these powers assert their limited or partial right as though it were absolute and cause a self-division and self-waste of spirit. For Hegel "mere suffering is not tragic, but only suffering that comes from a special kind of action. Pity for mere misfortune, like the fear of it, is not tragic pity or fear. These are due to the spectacle of the conflict and its attendant suffering, which do not appeal simply to our sensibilities or our instinct of self-preservation, but also to our deeper mind or spirit". Thus in *Paradise Lost* it is not mankind's suffering that resulted from the fall that is tragic, not the pity for the loss of the Garden, not even the fall itself; but rather the spiritual conflict of which the fall and its resultant suffering are the consequence. In other words, if we return to a distinction made earlier between evil and sin — that sin is the act of will, evil the consequence of sin — then it is sin that is tragic.

In *Paradise Lost* the spiritual conflict resolves itself at the moment of the fall into one between, on the one hand, the absolute obedience that should have been granted to God because of man's love for his creator; and, on the other, Adam's feeling for the "bond of nature" that links him with Eve. In Hegelian terms both of these are seen as "good in themselves", and the conflict between them "not so much the war of good with evil as the war of good with good". The next step in the theory, however, — that as a result of this conflict "the right of each is pushed into wrong" — is a more difficult one to relate to the poem, because of the natural tendency to identify Hegel's "ethical substance" with God; in which case the conflict inherent in the fall does not follow the Hegelian pattern of a collision of powers each of which is a partial manifestation of the total ethical substance. Rather the conflict becomes one between the ethical substance itself, as an absolute, and the particular manifestation, or part of it, the bond between man and wife.

Thus it may be true that the particular manifestation of God, the limited power, Adam's feeling for Eve, right in itself, becomes a wrong "because it ignores the right of the other and demands that absolute sway that does not belong to it alone, but to the whole of which it is a part". As regards Adam's duty to God, however, if God *is* the ethical substance itself, then this is something to which absolute sway *does* belong, and therefore it cannot be seen as being "pushed into wrong" by ignoring the claims of part of itself. But this is so only if the ethical substance is identified with God. If on the other hand we approach the poem from the point of view of a theoretical Christian humanism, then it might be argued that if this were a genuine attempt to fuse or balance its two elements, Christianity and humanism, then man's duty to God and his duty to himself as man would be of equal standing, and the "ethical substance" necessarily something which transcended or subsumed them both. The Hegelian formula would then apply, each side of the conflict being limited goods and the conflict between them one in which the right of each is pushed into wrong by the necessity imposed on Adam to choose between them.

Certainly in *Paradise Lost* the tragic conflict accords with Hegel's theory in that its outcome is "the denial of exclusive claims". At least for the time being the bond between man and God, and that between man and wife, is effectively broken. And one might want at least to surmise that the result might have been the same even had Adam chosen differently; that feelings of guilt at having abandoned Eve, of alienation from his human nature, would have marred the perfection of his bond with God. This immediate outcome Hegel sees as "the act of the ethical substance itself, asserting its absoluteness against the excessive pretensions of its particular powers"; as "absolute right" cancelling claims "based on right but pushed into wrong". As regards the longer range effects, Hegel sees three kinds of outcome to tragic conflict. Firstly, it may be that the ethical substance "reconciles by some adjustment the claims of the contending powers"; or the hero "by his own self-condemnation and inward purification reconciles himself with the supreme justice"; or, finally, the denial of the one sided or limited claims "involves the death of one or more of the persons concerned and we have a catastrophe".

All three of these resolutions have relevance for *Paradise Lost*, dependent on the view that is taken of the poem. The first may be seen as the Renaissance ideal of a reconciliation of the contending claims of Christianity and humanism. The fact that this ideal has not been fully realized, that it is, indeed, fundamentally unrealizable – that when Milton attempted such a reconciliation in *Paradise Regained* he failed – only serves to accentuate the tragic conflict. The next solution may depend on our taking the more deliberately Christian view of the tragic conflict as that of the limited good of man's duty to himself asserting itself against the absolute good of man's duty to God. In that case the process by which Adam and Eve move through self-condemnation and inward purification toward final reconciliation with God and with each other is clear enough. Finally, again from the straightforward Christian point of view at least, the fall, which "brought death into the world and all our woe", did undoubtedly lead to catastrophe. Though it might be noted that, again from the Christian point of view, it is not the denial but rather the affirmation by Adam of the "one-sided claim" of his humanity that results in the catastrophe. On the other hand, for the humanist the catastrophe may well be seen to stem from the denial of this claim by the opposite power of Adam's duty to God.

Where, as in this last view of *Paradise Lost*, there is catastrophe, the ethical substance may appear as a destructive force. However, Hegel would insist that it is not the rightful powers with which the combatants have identified themselves that are denied. On the contrary, "those powers, and with them the only thing for which the combatants cared, are affirmed. What is denied is the exclusive and therefore wrongful assertion of their right". Thus even where there is catastrophe Hegel insists that the end is not without an aspect of reconciliation. And certainly the close of *Paradise Lost* is reconciliatory rather than destructive in tone. The symbolic re-establishment of the bond between Adam and Eve as they leave the Garden is an eminently clear assertion of this spirit of reconciliation; and also, perhaps, it is an affirmation in Hegelian terms of those powers whose opposition had brought about the tragedy of the fall.

This Hegelian model of tragedy has, I think, a number of advantages as a way of looking at *Paradise Lost*. Firstly, the concept of tragedy based on the tragic flaw tended more or less to see this flaw as the *cause* of tragedy, the tragedy itself being rather seen as the consequences which result from the operation of the tragic flaw. In so far as this is the case, the result is to remove tragedy from the innermost life of the protagonist and move it, as it were, toward external events at its periphery. And this, of course, is much more so with the tragedy of circumstance, the tragedy induced by the operation of fate, or chance, or the gods. For Hegel, however, the tragedy is quite specifically the inner conflict between contending powers; as we have already seen, in relation to the fall it is the sin, the actual act of will, that is the tragedy, and not the evil that follows from it. And this is in keeping with the consistently inward movement of *Paradise Lost*, with its emphasis on the mind of man at its centre.

Secondly, the Hegelian model serves to overcome the problem of evil in the unfallen world, making evil the outcome of the fall, as indeed it had been in the original story, without its being the cause of it. This cause lies within Adam, but because the fall – that is, Adam's tragedy – is seen as a conflict of competing goods, the question of his having been created evil, or with the potentiality for evil, does not arise. Evil, as I have said, is the outcome of Adam's rejection of God, and neither the rejection itself nor its cause. And because Hegel's theory does not see Adam's action as wrong in itself, it makes more understandable our very real feeling of sympathy for him. Indeed, because it is a theory of tragedy rather than of morality, Hegel's concept does not call on us to decide whether Adam was right or wrong, to decide what it was his duty to do. The essence of tragedy for Hegel lies in the fact that "the acceptance of one power justified in itself should involve the violation of another similarly justified power". Accepting that Adam's duty to God and his duty to his own human nature were both "justified in themselves", then the question as to whether in the circumstances Adam's choice was morally right or wrong does not alter in any way the tragic quality of his situation. This depends simply on the existence of the conflict itself.

Finally, because it sees the choice facing Adam between his duty to God and his duty to himself not as one between good and evil but one between conflicting and competing goods, the Hegelian concept allows *Paradise Lost* to be set firmly in the context of the Christian humanist dilemma, and thereby brings to the forefront what to most present-day readers is likely to be its most absorbing aspect.

Despite these things, however, I would not want to suggest that *Paradise Lost* is simply an example of Hegelian tragedy, that it can be explained wholly in terms of this particular pattern. Indeed, each of the forms of tragedy, as we have seen, in its own way contributes something to an understanding of the poem. And, moreover, the process of attempting to fit Milton's narrative of the fall into these varying patterns of tragedy has itself been illuminating. I would not wish to dispense with any of the light that has thus been shed, for as I have said previously *Paradise Lost* is far too complex an organism to be understood completely from any single point of view.

9

The Ultimate Failure

Paradise Regained is the most personal of Milton's major poems. Its ideal of the Christian—humanist hero presented through the figure of Christ, the God become man, is also Milton's ideal of himself. But *Paradise Regained* is also the poem of Milton's old age — he was within a few years of his death when he wrote it, probably around 1668 — and its ideal is an austere one. So austere in fact, that it must be counted a failure, not as a poem but as an attempt to fuse the conflicting claims of Christianity and humanism. For though Christ fights and wins his battle against evil essentially as a man, with man's resources, ultimately he does so at the expense of his humanity.

Paradise Regained was clearly intended by Milton to be a sequel to *Paradise Lost*. The relationship is indicated by the opening lines:

> I who erewhile the happy garden sung,
> By one man's disobedience lost, now sing
> Recovered Paradise to all mankind,
> By one man's firm obedience fully tried
> Through all temptation, and the tempter foiled
> In all his wiles, defeated and repulsed,
> And Eden raised in the waste wilderness.   (*P.R.*, I, 1—7)

It is, however, a very different kind of poem; for many readers, indeed, a disconcertingly different one. It has none of the magnificence, the amplitude of *Paradise Lost*, and very little of its imaginative richness. A clue to this difference is generally accepted as having been provided by Milton himself in his *Reason for Church Government,* in which he writes of "that Epic form whereof the two poems of Homer, and those two of Virgil and Tasso are a diffuse, and the Book of Job a brief model . . ."[1] *Paradise Lost* then is an example of the "diffuse" epic, while with *Paradise Regained* Milton is seen as seeking to write a brief epic on the model of the Book of Job. This is no doubt a likely theory, but there are perhaps more compelling explanations for the form of the poem than simply a desire by the poet to write in accordance with the requirements of a particular form.

1. *The Reason of Church Government Urged against Prelaty* (1642); quoted from Douglas Bush, *op.cit.*, p. 126.

In the first place, the austerity of the ideal embodied in *Paradise Regained* would make the earlier poem an entirely inappropriate model. Such imaginative richness as *Paradise Regained* does have belongs as we shall see almost exclusively to Satan. But more immediately important, it is a genuine sequel, that is it carries on where *Paradise Lost* left off. And it will be remembered that the consistent inward movement of the earlier poem had by its close narrowed down its epic scope from the infinite immensity with which it began, to concentrate on the lonely figures of Adam and Eve as they leave the Garden to face the world beyond. Man is always the point of reference, is always at the centre of the stage in *Paradise Lost,* but by the end of the poem, as we have seen, he has become the stage. And this is the situation that is continued in *Paradise Regained.* Its drama is essentially one of an inner struggle, worked out within the mind of Christ, as man. Whereas the Garden before the fall had provided an environment completely in harmony with man, the desert for Christ is at best neutral, at worst hostile; in either case ensuring that Christ's struggle is concentrated entirely on himself.

In this same connection it is interesting, but not I think unexpected, that Milton should have chosen the relatively minor episode of the temptation in the wilderness as his subject for *Paradise Regained*, rather than what for most Christians would be the much more central episode of the crucifixion. Indeed this latter episode had been directly related to man's redemption both in the discussion between the Father and the Son in Book III of *Paradise Lost* and in Michael's final narrative, and it might therefore be seen as the logical subject for a sequel. In neither of these passages, in fact, is the episode of the temptation in the wilderness so much as mentioned. However, just as in *Paradise Lost* the fall had been the result of an inner conflict, of a struggle within the mind of man, so it is with his redemption. Although Milton acknowledges Christ's traditional role as redeemer, his need to pay man's debt by dying on the cross, what interests him is to depict Christ as an example which man can specifically follow towards achieving his own redemption — as one who shows the way to his, Milton's, ideal of kingship over the self, to the "inner paradise" promised by Michael to Adam at the end of *Paradise Lost.* For this purpose the temptation story was clearly the more suitable.

Finally, before going on to look at the poem itself, though the central figure of *Paradise Regained* is Christ, the poem begins, as does *Paradise Lost,* by putting the emphasis on man, on "one man's firm obedience fully tried" (*P.R.*, I, 4). In his portrayal of Christ in this poem, Milton had at his disposal a wide range of choices offered by the Christian tradition, from Christ virtually as God but for the time being assuming the guise and role of man, to the opposite extreme of him as essentially man, divine only in his origin and in his special mission. It is obvious that he would have chosen the latter end of this range, that he would present

Christ, with reference to *Paradise Lost* rather as the second Adam than as the Son of God of Book III or of the triumphant conclusion of the war in Heaven. It is for this reason that I have chosen not to use capitals for such words as "he", "his", etc., referring to Christ. Thus the parallel of the opening lines is between what has been "By one man's disobedience lost" and what will be recovered "By one man's firm obedience fully tried". Indeed, the true antecedents of the Christ of *Paradise Regained*, rather than the Son of *Paradise Lost*, are the so-called "types" of Christ — Abdiel, for instance, and Noah, whom Michael describes to Adam as

> . . . the only son of light
> In a dark age, against example good,
> Against allurement, custom, and a world
> Offended; fearless of reproach and scorn,
> Or violence, he of their wicked ways
> Shall them admonish, and before them set
> The paths of righteousness, how much more safe,
> And full of peace, denouncing wrath to come
> On their impenitence; and shall return
> Of them derided, but of God observed
> The one just man alive . . .   (*P.L.*, XI, 808–18)

This is not surprising, for even in *Paradise Lost* it is not difficult to believe that for Milton these, and not Adam or Satan, or even Christ himself, are the true heroes, those who most fully embody the ideal to which Milton fundamentally subscribed. Those, that is, who "dared to be singularly good" (*P.R.*, III, 57). This is perhaps very much as Milton had come to see himself after long years of involvement in political and religious controversy which, successful as it may have been at the time, must have seemed with the return of the King to have been ultimately ineffective — his one way of salvaging his own self-esteem.

It is essential for a correct reading of *Paradise Regained* that one understand the nature of the contest between Christ and Satan. Though traditionally it is a series of temptations, as Milton presents it this is not what it really is; or at least not all that it is. For one thing Christ never seems in any real danger of succumbing, so that simply as temptations the episodes are lacking in dramatic tension. What we wonder about as Satan makes his various offers to Christ is not whether Christ will escape but how he will go about it, what answers he will find. And this seems indeed to be the nature of Christ's trial: not to escape temptation but to find the right reasons for doing so, and in the process to learn more about himself and his mission. Speaking to Gabriel of Christ, God says that

> . . . first I mean
> To exercise him in the wilderness,
> There he shall first lay down the rudiments
> Of his great warfare, ere I send him forth
> To conquer Sin and Death . . .   (*P.R.*, I, 155–59)

And Christ himself speaks of how

> . . . by some strong motion I am led
> Into this wilderness, to what intent
> I learn not yet, perhaps I need not know;
> For what concerns my knowledge God reveals.   (*P.R.*, I, 290–93)

Christ knows that he is the Son of God, that he is the promised Messiah, and he has already thought a great deal about his destiny and how it is to be accomplished. But the full meaning of these things is not yet clear to him. On the other hand, neither are they clear to his opponent, Satan. Indeed, the basic tension of their coming struggle derives from the fact that though both know that Christ is the Son of God neither is fully aware of what this means.

Both Christ and Satan need to know who Christ really is; Christ himself in order that he may know the true nature of his mission, and Satan that he may know the nature of the threat, if any, which Christ presents to the dominion over man that Satan had won at the fall. The contest is not so much one which will lead to Christ's victory over Satan or *vice versa*, but one which will lay down the nature of their "great warfare" in time to come. In the meanwhile, Satan, for instance, obviously does not know that this is the same Son of God who was responsible for his summary expulsion from Heaven. "And what will he not do to advance his son?" he asks, speaking of God:

> His first-begot we know, and sore have felt,
> When his fierce thunder drove us to the deep;
> Who this is we must learn . . .   (*P.R.*, I, 89–91)

The question of what it means to be Son of God, in fact, runs right through the poem, providing the tension as Christ seeks to learn the answer and Satan tries to trick him into revealing it. "Who this is we must learn" Satan tells his followers at the beginning, and just before the final temptation he makes clear the real purpose behind his efforts. " . . . Son of God to me is yet in doubt" he tells Christ, and therefore

> . . . I thought thee worth my nearer view
> And narrower scrutiny, that I might learn
> In what degree or meaning thou art called
> The Son of God, which bears no single sense;
> The Son of God I also am, or was,
> And if I was, I am; relation stands;
> All men are Sons of God . . .   (*P.R.*, IV, 514–20)

Here Satan's assertion that he too is the Son of God, that indeed all men are Sons of God, serves to retain the central position of man and to strengthen the identification of Christ with man.

The whole episode is thus for Christ a process of self-discovery in which Satan, while seeking to defend himself by learning who and what this new potential enemy is, unwittingly serves God's purpose by assisting Christ towards self-knowledge as he works out the right answer to each so-called temptation. And in this sense, too, *Paradise Regained* is a continuation of what had happened in *Paradise Lost*, where we have seen the fall and the events that followed it to be a similar pattern of self-discovery and self-understanding. The angels greet God's statement of his plan for His Son with the words:

> Victory and triumph to the Son of God
> Now ent'ring his great duel, not of arms,
> But to vanquish by wisdom hellish wiles.   (*P.R.*, I, 173–75)

It is to gain this wisdom, rather than simply to overcome temptation that Christ is sent into the wilderness.

This process of discovery begins even before Christ's entry into the wilderness. The search is in fact introduced by Satan and his henchmen who, from the splendour of the great council in Pandemonium, have been reduced to a "gloomy consistory" meeting somewhere in the clouds above the earth. Satan has witnessed Christ's meeting with John the Baptist and knows from this that he is someone chosen by God and thus a potential threat to him and his followers. Then we listen to a long soliloquy from Christ himself in which he outlines his own search to discover the meaning of the signs he has been given:

> When I was yet a child, no childish play
> To me was pleasing, all my mind was set
> Serious to learn and know, and thence to do
> What might be public good; myself I thought
> Born to that end, born to promote all truth,
> All righteous things ...   (*P.R.*, I, 201–6)

Perhaps the most interesting aspect of this process of self-discovery thus far is that Christ has already, very early in his search, dismissed physical force as a means of realizing his mission:

> ... yet this not all
> To which my spirit aspired, victorious deeds
> Flamed in my heart, heroic acts, one while
> To rescue Israel from the Roman yoke,
> Thence to subdue and quell o'er all the earth
> Brute violence and proud tyrannic power,
> Till truth were freed, and equity restored;
> Yet held it more humane, more heavenly first
> By winning words to conquer willing hearts,
> And make persuasion do the work of fear.   (*P.R.*, I, 214–23)

Christ has thus already passed the point of understanding reached by the angels at the time of Satan's rebellion, as to the means by which good is able to combat evil.

The temptations offered to Christ in the poem follow only in a fairly general way those of the Biblical narrative. The first is the traditional one of turning the stones into bread. As Milton presents it this is ostensibly a temptation of faith; of Christ's faith, that is, that God will provide whatever is needful to him. But it can also be read as an attempt by Satan to lead Christ into revealing himself, to show whether in fact he can turn the stones into bread; an attempt which ironically leads not to a greater understanding on the part of Satan, but to a growth of Christ's knowledge, specifically regarding Satan's identity. Christ's reply to Satan's suggestion that " . . . if thou be the Son of God command / That out of these hard stones be made thee bread", sets a dramatic pattern that will become familiar in the poem:

> Think'st thou such force in bread? Is it not written
> (For I discern thee other than thou seem'st)
> Man lives not by bread alone, but each word
> Proceeding from the mouth of God; who fed
> Our fathers here with manna . . .
> Why dost thou then suggest to me distrust,
> Knowing who I am, as I know who thou art?   (*P.R.*, I, 347–56)

In fact Satan knows no more about Christ than he knew before, but Christ's understanding both of himself and of the identity of his antagonist has been advanced. Here, as throughout the poem, we feel that Christ approaches the problem as man, with man's limited resources, and finally reaches, or is granted, a further apparently intuitive insight; in this case in what seems to come as just such an insight, an understanding of who and what he is up against. In other words, in this episode, as throughout *Paradise Regained*, we are seeing Christ not only as man but as "fallen" man, striving successfully to regain some of the intuitive knowledge of good lost at the fall. The process is, indeed, parallel to that we have seen operating in relation to will and grace. Just as man must will his own redemption in order to gain access to God's grace, so he must go as far as he can by his own human power of discursive reasoning before gaining the additional insight to know good directly.

Having been discovered, Satan counters by offering to help Christ, just as he had, he claims, helped God when, for instance, " . . . he / Gave up into my hands Uzzean Job / To prove him . . . " (*P.R.*, I, 368–70). But Christ escapes this trap easily by his understanding that though God may make use of evil as part of his providence, this is for God to decide and not for evil thereby to claim to be useful to God. So that when Satan offers to follow him in his mission Christ with "unaltered brow" replies:

> Thy coming hither, though I know thy scope,
> I bid not nor forbid; do as thou find'st
> Permission from above; thou canst not more.   (*P.R.*, I, 494–96)

Christ is indeed already showing himself a difficult opponent for Satan,
holding him easily at arms length, as it were, refusing to become involved
in his blandishments. And at the beginning of the second book we are
given what may be an important clue as to why he is able to do this.

Firstly, we are introduced to Mary, the mother of Christ, the second
Eve, whose seed as we learned from Michael at the end of *Paradise Lost*
was destined to "bruise the heel" of Satan. But it is clear that, unlike the
first Eve in the earlier poem, Mary is to play no active role in the events
of *Paradise Regained*. As she awaits his return from the wilderness she
remembers the events of his childhood, up to the time

> . . . when twelve years he scarce had seen,
> I lost him, but so found, as well I saw,
> He could not lose himself; but went about
> His Father's business; what he meant I mused,
> Since understand; much more his absence now
> Thus long to some great purpose he obscures.
> But I to wait with patience am inured;
> My heart hath been a storehouse long of things
> And sayings laid up, portending strange events.
> .   .   .   .   .
> The while her son tracing the desert wild
> Sole but with holiest meditations fed,
> Into himself descended . . .   (*P.R.*, II, 96—111)

Mary's passive role is given significance in the following scene when the
frustrated Satan returns to his fellow demons seeking advice. The task,
he tells them, will be far more difficult

> Than when I dealt with Adam first of men,
> Though Adam by his wife's allurement fell,
> However to this man inferior far . . .   (*P.R.*, II, 133—35)

And when Belial — whom we will remember from *Paradise Lost* as one
than whom "a fairer person lost not heaven" (*P.L.*, II, 110), but who has
now become " . . . the dissolutest spirit that fell, / The sensualest . . . / The
fleshliest incubus" (*P.R.*, II, 150—52) — advises Satan to "Set women in
his eye and in his walk", he is quickly told that " . . . in much uneven scale
thou weighst / All others by thyself" (*P.R.*, II, 173—74). "He whom we
attempt is wiser far / Than Solomon, of more exalted mind" Satan
declares. Should any woman, as Venus had once done with Jove, seek to
enamour him,

> How would one look from his majestic brow
> Seated as on top of virtue's hill,
> Discount'nance her despised, and put to rout
> All her array; her female pride deject,
> Or turn to reverent awe! For beauty stands

In the admiration only of weak minds
Led captive . . .
Therefore with manlier objects we must try
His constancy . . .   (*P.R.*, II, 216–26)

With Mary left firmly at home, with Christ alone in the wilderness "into himself descended", the weakness which Eve represented for the first Adam is not to be feared; but if this is so what of the share of Adam's humanity she represented, what of the fact that without her Adam was incomplete, "barren".

Returning to the wilderness after the conference with his fellows, Satan sets before Christ a sumptuous repast. This is one of the few richly imaginative passages in the poem. Indeed in this largely austere work all the richness, almost all the overt imagery, certainly all the sensuousness is given to Satan. The "pleasant grove, / With chant of tuneful birds resounding loud; . . . High roofed . . . " suggests the Church, which makes ironic the continued description:

Nature's own work it seemed (Nature taught Art)
And to a superstitious eye the haunt
Of wood-gods and wood-nymphs . . .   (*P.R.*, II, 289–97)

And in fact the whole elaborate scene becomes Milton's satiric comment on the material richness of the Church:

A table richly spread, in regal mode,
With dishes piled, and meats of noblest sort
And savour, beasts of chase, or fowl of game,
In pastry built, or from the spit, or boiled,
Grisamber-steamed, all fish from sea or shore,
Freshet, or purling brook, of shell or fin,
And exquisitest name, for which was drained
Pontus and Lucrine bay, and Afric coast.
Alas how simple, to these cates compared
Was that crude apple that diverted Eve!   (*P.R.*, II, 340–49)

In response to Satan's invitation to "sit down and eat" Christ neatly turns Satan's own argument of the previous temptation against him:

Said'st thou not that to all things I had right?
And who withholds my power that right to use?
Shall I receive by gift what of my own,
When and where likes me best, I can command?

And with the same impression of insight, of intuitive understanding as on the previous occasion:

I can at will, doubt not, as soon as thou,
Command a table in this wilderness.   (*P.R.*, II, 379–84)

Against the background richness of the Satanic "table", this becomes a rather beautiful statement of the right of the individual to set up his own table, to make his own communion direct with God, independent of the elaborate trappings of the earthly church.

Having failed with hunger, Satan turns to the temptation of riches, specifically as a means of enabling Christ to gain the throne of Judah. Christ scornfully rejects his offer, of both "riches and realms"; and he goes on to speak of the "office of a king" as being "That for the public all this weight he bears". Yet, he says,

> . . . he who reigns with himself, and rules
> Passions, desires, and fears, is more a king;
> Which every wise and virtuous man attains:
> And who attains not, ill aspires to rule
> Cities of men, or headstrong multitudes,
> Subject himself to anarchy within,
> Or lawless passions in him which he serves.   (*P.R.*, II, 466—72)

We are back to the theme of self-enthralment which began with Satan's rebellion against God, and we are reminded of Abdiel's words at that time:

> . . . This is servitude,
> To serve the unwise, or him who hath rebelled
> Against his worthier, as thine now serve thee,
> Thy self not free, but to thy self enthralled.   (*P.L.*, VI, 178—81)

The need for self-sufficiency, for individual autonomy, for kingship over the self from now on becomes central to the narrative in *Paradise Regained*, as Christ rejects each successive temptation at least partly on the ground that such things as wealth, power, glory, learning are so many invitations to self-enthralment, to the surrender of self-sufficiency to the need for external things.

The next temptation offered by Satan is in fact that of glory, of fame. "These godlike virtues wherefore doest thou hide?" he asks,

> Affecting private life, or more obscure
> In savage wilderness, wherefore deprive
> All earth her wonder at thy acts, thyself
> The fame and glory, glory the reward
> That sole excites to high attempts the flame
> Of most erected spirits . . .   (*P.R.*, III, 21—27)

But this invitation to make himself dependent on public reputation brings out the fierce independence of Christ, or more accurately perhaps of Milton:

> For what is glory but the blaze of fame,
> The people's praise, if always praise unmixed?
> And what the people but a herd confused,
> A miscellaneous rabble, who extol
> Things vulgar, and well weighed, scarce worth the praise,

They praise and they admire they know not what;
And know not whom, but as one leads the other;
And what delight to be by such extolled,
To live upon their tongues and be their talk,
Of whom to be dispraised were no small praise?
His lot who dares to be singularly good.

.　　　.　　　.　　　.　　　.

This is true glory and renown, when God
Looking on the earth, with approbation marks
The just man . . .　　　(*P.R.*, III, 47–62)

Readers familiar with Milton's *Lycidas* will very likely feel an echo here of the reference to "fame" in that poem:

Fame is the spur that the clear spirit doth raise
(That last infirmity of noble mind)
To scorn delights and live laborious days;
But the fair guerdon when we hope to find,
And think to burst out into sudden blaze,
Comes the blind Fury with the abhorred shears
And slits the thin-spun life . . .　　　(*Lycidas*, 70–76)

And there is a message even perhaps for the twentieth century in Christ's castigation of the seekers after "false glory":

They err who count it glorious to subdue
By conquest far and wide, to overrun
Large countries, and in field great battles win,
Great cities by assault: what do these worthies,
But rob and spoil, burn, slaughter, and enslave
Peaceable nations, neighbouring, or remote,
Made captive, yet deserving freedom more
Than those their conquerors, who leave behind
Nothing but ruin wheresoe'er they rove,
And all the flourishing works of peace destroy,
Then swell with pride, and must be titled gods,
Great benefactors of mankind . . .　　　(*P.R.*, III, 71–82)

Satan's next effort is to take Christ to the top of a high mountain from whence he can see, among other things, the ten enslaved tribes of Israel. Satan's offer of help in freeing these tribes is rejected by Christ, on the ground that their slavery is only an outward sign of their lack of inner freedom:

As for those captive tribes, themselves were they
Who wrought their own captivity, fell off
From God to worship calves . . .

.　　　.　　　.　　　.

Should I of these the liberty regard,
Who freed, as to their ancient patrimony,

Unhumbled, unrepentent, unreformed
Headlong would follow and to their gods perhaps
Of Bethel and of Dan? No, let them serve
Their enemies, who serve idols with God.   (*P.R.,* III, 414–32)

If the tribes are to be freed, then it will be in God's time, and for Christ
"To his due time and providence I leave them". By this time I suspect
that many present-day readers will begin to feel a lack of warmth, of
human feeling, even of Christian charity in Milton's Christ. And it is with
something of the same spirit that Christ meets Satan's next offer, that
of the glories of imperial Rome. Not that this is difficult for him, for it is
the degenerate Rome of the Emperor Tiberius that he is offered, with as
he says "Their sumptuous feasts and gorgeous gluttonies", and he bitingly
turns the offer back on Satan:

. . . I shall, thou say'st, expel
A brutish monster: what if I withal
Expel a devil who first made him such?   (*P.R.,* IV, 127–29)

And he returns once again to the theme of freedom and the absolute need
for inner freedom if outward freedom is to be possible. "Let his tormentor
conscience find him out" he says of Tiberius:

For him I was not sent, nor yet to free
That people victor once, now vile and base,
Deservedly made vassal . . .
What wise and valiant man would seek to free
These thus degenerate, by themselves enslaved,
Or could of inward slaves made outward free?   (*P.R.,* IV, 130–34)

Following this rebuff Satan, like the good salesman he is, tries making
the goods seem more attractive by raising the price. What he is next to
offer carries the condition that Christ should "fall down / And worship me
as thy superior lord" (*P.R.,* IV, 166–67). He is rejected by Christ's
brusque "I never liked thy talk, thy offers less", but still persists. What he
now offers Christ is nothing less than the learning and literature of Greece.
He tells Christ that "with the Gentiles much thou must converse", and

Without their learning how wilt thou with them,
Or they with thee hold conversation meet?
How wilt thou reason with them, how refute
Their idolisms, traditions, paradoxes?   (*P.R.,* IV, 229–34)

After alluding to Greek poetry and eloquence he turns to the Greek
philosophical schools as a source of just that inner strength emphasized
by Christ himself. Their rules, he says, "will render thee a king complete /
Within thyself, much more with empire joined" (*P.R.,* IV, 282–83). But
this too is rejected:

> . . . many books
> Wise men have said are wearisome; who reads
> Incessantly, and to his reading brings not
> A spirit and judgment equal or superior,
>
> .   .   .   .   .
>
> Deep versed in books and shallow in himself,
> Crude or intoxicate, collecting toys,
> And trifles for choice matters worth a sponge;
> As children gathering pebbles on the shore.   (*P.R.*, IV, 321–30)

Admittedly this is Christ speaking, not Milton. But we have seen how much of Milton himself has gone into his portrayal of Christ, and if we remember the long period of his life that Milton had devoted to reading and study, particularly to the reading and study of just that classical learning he is now rejecting, the form of this temptation and of Christ's rejection of it must seem surprising to say the least. Can we accept that Milton, one of the greatest of classical scholars, sincerely believed what he has Christ say about Hebrew literature:

> . . . if I would delight my private hours
> With music or with poem, where so soon
> As in our native language can I find
> That solace? All our Law and story strewed
> With hymns, our psalms with artful terms inscribed,
> Our Hebrew songs and harps in Babylon,
> That pleased so well our victor's ear, declare
> That rather Greece from us these arts derived;
> Ill imitated, while they loudest sing
> The vices of their deities . . .   (*P.R.*, IV, 331–40)

It is almost as though Milton had asked himself what was the greatest sacrifice he could think of making in the interest of self-autonomy, of kingship over the self; and certainly it is significant that in these two last temptations he has Christ reject both Greece and Rome, the twin bases of the classical heritage of western Christiandom, of the humanist side of the Christian—humanist dichotomy.

This rejection is given point by what is probably an unconsciously humorous episode that follows. Satan, apparently in an effort to "soften up" Christ for a final assault, sends an horrific overnight thunderstorm:

> . . . either tropic now
> 'Gan thunder, and both ends of heaven, the clouds
> From many a horrid rift abortive poured
> Fierce rain with lightning mixed, water with fire
> In ruin reconciled: nor slept the winds
> Within their stony caves, but rushed abroad
> From the four hinges of the world, and fell
> On the vexed wilderness . . .   (*P.R.*, IV, 409–16)

But when Satan seeks out Christ in the morning, no doubt hoping to find him reduced to a quivering jelly, he is greeted with what might seem to be one of the worst lines in English, or any other poetry, but which in its complete flatness, its lack of any imaginative quality, may in fact be quite appropriate to the situation:

> Me worse than wet thou find'st not . . .   (*P.R.*, IV, 486)

Christ is not terrified because to be terrified would require some imagination, some human feeling, and this we have come reluctantly to realize he is lacking. The significance of the absence of Mary, the second Eve, is now apparent. Christ, the second Adam, from the point of view of human sensitivity, of common humanity, is indeed "barren", achieving the promised inner paradise of self-sufficiency by the rejection of that part of himself that had proved the weakness of the first Adam, but which was none the less an essential part of his human nature.

Satan's final attempt is, of course, to place Christ on the pinnacle of the temple, apparently with a view to having him revealed once and for all as the Son of God; or, if he is not, of seeing him killed in the fall to the ground. After the thunderstorm episode it is not surprising that Christ continues to frustrate Satan by simply standing where he is, with the enigmatic response: "Tempt not the Lord thy God". Is he saying that Satan should not tempt him to reveal himself, or that he, Christ, should not himself tempt God by placing his life in His hands in this way? It might be noted that on this occasion Christ's response is immediate; he no longer seems to need the process of rationalizing the situation before reaching his final insight. So that it is time for the angelic chorus to declare

> . . . on thy glorious work
> Now enter and begin to save mankind.   (*P.R.*, IV, 634–35)

But in keeping with its consistent emphasis on Christ as man, the poem ends on a quiet note: "He unobserved, / Home to his mother's house private returned". The reader will, I think, inevitably feel the narrowing of vision between this and the magnificence, the human challenge, of the ending of *Paradise Lost*. *Paradise Regained* is a fascinating poem, but it does not show the way to any really satisfactory resolution of the conflicts and paradoxes inherent in the image of the human condition presented to us by *Paradise Lost*.

Select Bibliography

The Milton literature is second in magnitude only to that of Shakespeare and the following lists are necessarily selective. The Bibliography has been divided into: (a) editions, including some early as well as modern works; (b) biography; (c) general reference; (d) background, divided into (i) primary and (ii) secondary works; (e) critical monographs; and (f) critical articles.

EDITIONS

(in chronological order)

Poetical Works of Milton. Annotations by P[atrick] H[ume]. London, 1695.

Paradise Lost. A Poem in Twelve Books, ed. Thomas Newton *et al.* 3rd ed. 2 vols. London: J. & R. Tonson, 1749.

The Poetical Works of John Milton, ed. Henry John Todd *et al.* 3rd ed. 7 vols. London: J. Johnson, etc., 1809.

The Paradise Lost of Milton. [With Illustrations, designed and engraved by John Martin.] London: Septimus Prowett, 1827.

The Poetical Works of John Milton, ed. David Masson. 3 vols. London: Macmillan, 1874.

Paradise Lost. [Illustrations by William Blake.] Liverpool: Lyceum Press, 1906.

The Works of John Milton, ed. Frank Allen Patterson *et al.* 18 vols. New York: Columbia University Press, 1931–38.

The Student's Milton, ed. Frank Allen Patterson, 2nd ed. New York: Appleton-Century-Crofts, 1933.

John Milton. Complete Poems and Major Prose, ed. Merritt Y. Hughes. New York: Odyssey Press, 1957.

The Essential Milton, ed. Douglas Bush. 1949; rpt. London: Chatto & Windus, n.d.

John Milton. Paradise Lost and Paradise Regained, ed. Christopher Ricks. New York: Signet, 1968.

The Poems of John Milton, ed. John Carey and Alastair Fowler. London: Longmans, 1968.

BIOGRAPHY

Darbishire, Helen, ed. *The Early Lives of Milton.* London: Constable, 1932.
Masson, David. *The Lift of John Milton: Narrated in Connection with the Political, Ecclesiastical and Literary History of his Times.* 7 vols. Cambridge and London: Macmillan, 1859–94.
Parker, William Riley. *Milton. A Biography.* 2 vols. Oxford: Clarendon Press, 1968.

GENERAL REFERENCE

Hunter, William B., Jr., Shawcross, John T., Steadman, John M. *et al.,* ed. *A Milton Encyclopedia.* 8 vols. Lewisburg, Pa.: Bucknell University Press, 1978.
Johnson, William C. *Milton Criticism: A Subject Index.* Folkestone, Kent: Dawson, 1978.

BACKGROUND

(i) PRIMARY

The Bible (incl. *Apocrypha*)
The works of:
  Aeschylus; John Aubrey (*Brief Lives*); Saint Augustine (esp. *City of God*, Book XIV); Calvin; Camoens (*The Lusiads*); Dante; Dubartas; Euripides; Giles and Phineas Fletcher; Hesiod; Homer; Giovanno Francesco Loredano (*The Life of Adam*, 1640, ed. Roy C. Flannagan and John Arthos, Gainesville, Fla. Scolar Press, 1967); Lucan (*Pharsalia*); Origen; Ovid; Plato; Shakespeare; Sophocles; Spenser; Tasso; Virgil.
Collections of primary material:

Haller, W., *Tracts on Liberty in the Puritan Revolution.* 3 vols. New York: Columbia University Press, 1933.

Haller, W. & Davies, G. ed., *The Leveller Tracts of 1647–1653.* New York: Columbia University Press, 1944.

Lamont, William and Oldfield, Sybil, eds., *Politics, Religion and Literature in the Seventeenth Century.* London: J. M. Dent, 1975.

Wolfe, D. M. *Leveller Manifestoes of the Puritan Revolution.* New York: Nelson, 1944.

(ii) SECONDARY

Arthos, John. *Milton and the Italian Cities.* London: Bowes & Bowes, 1968.

Bowra, C. M. *From Virgil to Milton.* London: Macmillan, 1943.

Brown, Eleanor. *Milton's Blindness.* New York: Columbia University Press, 1934.

Bush, Douglas. *Mythology and the Renaissance Tradition in English Poetry.* New revised ed. New York: W. W. Norton & Co, 1963.

Clark, Donald. *Milton at St. Paul's School.* New York: Columbia University Press, 1948.

Gilbert, Allan H., ed. *Literary Criticism: Plato to Dryden.* 1940; rpt. Detroit: Wayne State University Press, 1962.

Greene, Thomas. *The Descent from Heaven: A Study in Epic Continuity.* New Haven and London: Yale University Press, 1963.

Haller, William. *The Rise of Puritanism.* 1938; rpt. New York: Harper Torchbooks, 1957.

Hamilton, K. G. *The Two Harmonies: Poetry and Prose in the Seventeenth Century.* Oxford: Clarendon Press, 1963.

Hanford, James Holly. *A Milton Handbook.* 4th ed. New York: Appleton-Century-Crofts, 1954.

Hardison, O. B., Jr., ed. *English Literary Criticism: The Renaissance.* New York: Appleton-Century-Crofts, 1963.

Heninger, S. K., Jr. *The Cosmographical Glass: Renaissance Diagrams of the Universe.* San Marino, Calif.: The Huntington Library, 1977.

Highet, Gilbert. *The Classical Tradition: Greek and Roman Influences on Western Literature.* New York: O.U.P., 1949.

Hoopes, Robert. *Right Reason in the Renaissance.* Cambridge, Mass.: Harvard University Press, 1962.

Kirkconnell, Watson. *The Celestial Cycle: The Theme of Paradise Lost in World Literature, with Translations of the Major Analogues.* Toronto: University of Toronto Press, 1952.

Koestler, Arthur. *The Sleepwalkers. A History of Man's Changing Vision of the Universe.* 1959; rpt. Harmondsworth, Middlesex: Penguin Books, 1964.

Maclure, Millar. *The Paul's Cross Sermons 1534–1642.* London: University of Toronto Press, 1958.

Mahood, M. M. *Poetry and Humanism.* London: Cape, 1950.

Mitchell, W. Fraser. *English Pulpit Oratory from Andrewes to Tillotson.* London, 1932.

Nicolson, Marjorie Hope. *The Breaking of the Circle: Studies in the Effect of the "New Science" upon Seventeenth-Century Poetry.* Revised ed. New York: Columbia University Press, 1960.

———. *Science and Imagination.* Ithaca: Cornell University Press, 1956.

Smith, Alan G. R. *Science and Society in the Sixteenth and Seventeenth Centuries.* London: Thames & Hudson, 1972.

Thomas, Keith. *Religion and the Decline of Magic: Studies in Popular Beliefs in Sixteenth- and Seventeenth-Century England.* 1971; rpt. Harmondsworth, Middlesex: Penguin Books, 1978.

Trevelyan, G. M. *England under the Stuarts.* London: Methuen, 1965.

Wedgewood, C. V. *Milton and his World.* London: Lutterworth Press, 1969.

Weinberg, Bernard. *A History of Literary Criticism in the Italian Renaissance.* 2 vols. Chicago: Univ. of Ch. Press, 1961.

Willey, Basil. *The Seventeenth Century Background.* 1934; rpt. Garden City, N.Y.: Doubleday & Co, 1953.

Woodhouse, A. S. P., ed. *Puritanism and Liberty. Being the Army Debates (1647–49) from the Clarke Manuscripts with Supplementary Documents.* 2nd ed. London: J. M. Dent & Sons, 1974.

CRITICAL MONOGRAPHS

Addison, Joseph. *Criticisms on Paradise Lost,* ed. Albert S. Cook. New York, 1926.

Broadbent, J. B. *Some Graver Subject: An Essay on Paradise Lost.* 1960; rpt. New York: Schocken Books, 1967.

Burden, Dennis H. *The Logical Epic: A Study of the Argument of Paradise Lost.* London: Routledge & Kegan Paul, 1967.

Daniells, Roy. *Milton, Mannerism and Baroque.* Toronto: University of Toronto Press, 1963.

Duncan, Joseph E. *Milton's Earthly Paradise.* Minneapolis: University of Minnesota Press, 1972.

Empson, William. *Milton's God.* Revised ed. 1961; rpt. London: Chatto and Windus, 1965.

Evans, J. M. *Paradise Lost and the Genesis Tradition.* Oxford: Clarendon Press, 1968.

Ferry, Anne Davidson. *Milton's Epic Voice: the Narrator in Paradise Lost.* Cambridge, Mass.: Harvard University Press, 1963.

Fish, Stanley E. *Surprised by Sin: the Reader in Paradise Lost.* New York: St Martin's Press, 1967.

Frye, Northrop. *The Return of Eden: Five Essays on Milton's Epics.* Toronto: University of Toronto Press, 1965.

Frye, Roland Mushat. *Milton's Imagery and the Visual Arts: Iconographic Tradition in the Epics Poems.* Princeton: Princeton University Press, 1978.

Harding, Davis P. *The Club of Hercules: Studies in the Classical Background of Paradise Lost.* Urbana: University of Illinois Press, 1962.

Hill, Christopher. *Milton and the English Revolution.* London: Faber & Faber, 1977.

Hughes, Merritt Y. *Ten Perspectives on Milton.* New Haven, Conn.: Yale University Press, 1965.

Kelly, Maurice. *This Great Argument: a Study of Milton's De Doctrina Christiana as a Gloss upon Paradise Lost.* Princeton, New Jersey: Princeton University Press, 1941.

Lewalski, Barbara Kiefer. *Milton's Brief Epic: The Genre, Meaning, and Art of Paradise Regained.* Providence: Brown University Press, 1966.

MacCaffrey, Isabel Gamble. *Paradise Lost as "Myth".* Cambridge, Mass.: Harvard University Press, 1959.

Mahood, Margaret. *Poetry and Humanism.* London: Cape, 1950.

Martz, Louis L. *The Paradise Within: Studies in Vaughan, Traherne, and Milton.* New Haven & London, 1964.

Patrides, C. A. *Milton and the Christian Tradition.* Oxford: Clarendon Press, 1966.

Pointon, Marcia. *Milton and English Art.* Manchester: Manchester University Press, 1970.

Pope, Elizabeth M. *Paradise Regained: The Tradition and the Poem.* Baltimore: The Johns Hopkins Press, 1947.

Prince, F. T. *The Italian Element in Milton's Verse.* Oxford: Clarendon Press, 1954.

Ricks, Chistopher. *Milton's Grand Style.* Oxford: Clarendon Press, 1963.

Sims, James H. *The Bible in Milton's Epics.* Gainesville: University of Florida Press, 1962.

Steadman, John. *Epic and Tragic Structure in Paradise Lost.* Chicago: University of Chicago Press, 1976.

———. *Milton and the Renaissance Hero.* Oxford: Clarendon Press, 1967.

Stein, Arnold. *Answerable Style: Essays on Paradise Lost.* Minneapolis: University of Minnesota Press, 1953.

———. *Heroic Knowledge: An Interpretation of Paradise Regained and Samson Agonistes.* Minneapolis: University of Minnesota Press, 1957.

Summers, Joseph H. *The Muse's Method: An Introduction to Paradise Lost.* 1962; rpt. New York: W. W. Norton and Co, 1968.

Svendsen, Kester. *Milton and Science.* Cambridge, Mass.: Harvard University Press, 1956.

Thorpe, James E., Jr. *Milton Criticism: Selections from Four Centuries.* London: Rinehart and Co, 1950.

Tillyard, E. M. W. *Milton.* Revised ed. 1966; rpt. Harmondsworth, Middlesex: Penguin Books, 1968.

Waldock, A. J. A. *Paradise Lost and its Critics.* 1947; rpt. Cambridge: Cambridge University Press, 1966.

Webber, Joan. *Milton and his Epic Tradition.* University of Washington Press, 1979.

Wittreich, Joseph Anthony, J. *Angel of Apocalypse: Blake's Idea of Milton.* Madison, Wis.: University of Wisconsin Press, 1975.

———. *Visionary Poetics: Milton and his Legacy.* San Marino, Calif.: Huntington Library Press, 1979.

CRITICAL ARTICLES

Barker, Arthur E. "Structural Pattern in *Paradise Lost*", *Philological Quarterly* 28 (1949), rpt. in *Milton. Modern Essays in Criticism,* ed. Arthur E. Barker (London: Oxford University Press, 1965), pp. 142–55.

Bell, Millicent. "The Fallacy of the Fall in *Paradise Lost*", *Proceedings of the Modern Language Association of America,* 68 (1953), 863–83.

Blackburn, Thomas H. "Paradises Lost and Found: the Meaning and Function of the 'Paradise Within' in *Paradise Lost*", *Milton Studies* 5, ed. James D. Simmonds (Pittsburgh: Pittsburgh University Press, 1973), pp. 191–212.

Chambers, A. B. "Chaos in *Paradise Lost*", *Journal of the History of Ideas,* 24 (1963), 55 -84.

Cirillo, Albert R. "Noon–Midnight and the Temporal Structure of *Paradise Lost*", *English Literary History,* 29 (1962), 372–95.

Daiches, David. "The Opening of *Paradise Lost*", in *The Living Milton,* ed. Frank Kermode (London: Routledge, 1960), pp. 55–69.

Fish, Stanley Eugene. "Discovery as Form in *Paradise Lost*", *New Essays on Paradise Lost,* ed. Thomas Kranidas (Berkeley and Los Angeles: University of California Press, 1969), pp. 1–14.

Frye, Northrop. "The typology of *Paradise Regained*", *Modern Philology,* 53 (1956), 227–38, rpt. in Barker, *Modern Essays,* pp. 429–46.

Gardner, Helen. "Milton's Satan and the Theme of Damnation in Elizabethan Tragedy", *Essays and Studies,* New Series. 1 (1948), 46–66, rpt. in Barker, *Modern Essays,* pp. 205–17.

Gilbert, Allan H. "Milton on the Position of Women", *Modern Language Review,* 15 (1920), 240–64.

Hunter, William B., Jr. "Milton on the Exaltation of the Son: the War in Heaven in *Paradise Lost*", *English Literary History,* 36 (1969), 215–31.

Kermode, Frank. "Adam Unparadised", in *The Living Milton,* ed. Frank Kermode (London: Routledge, 1960), pp. 85–123.

Landy, Marcia. " 'A Free and Open Encounter': Milton and the Modern Reader", *Milton Studies*, 9 (1976), 3–36.

Lewalski, Barbara. "Innocence and Experience in Milton's Eden", *New Essays on Paradise Lost*, pp. 86–117.

———. "Milton on Women – Yet once More", *Milton Studies*, 6 (1974), pp. 3–20.

MacCaffrey, Isabel G. "The Theme of *Paradise Lost*, Book III", *New Essays on Paradise Lost*, pp. 58–85.

Mohl, Ruth. "Milton and the Idea of Perfection", in Ruth Mohl, *Studies in Spenser, Milton, and the Theory of Monarchy*. (New York: Columbia University Press, 1949), pp. 94–132.

Patrides, C. A. "Renaissance and Modern Views of Hell", *Harvard Theological Review*, 72 (1964), 217–36.

Prince, F. T. "On the Last Two Books of *Paradise Lost*", *Essays and Studies*, 11 (1958), 38–52.

Samuel, Irene. "The Development of Milton's Poetics", *Proceedings of the Modern Language Association of America*, 92 (1977), 231–40.

———. "The Dialogue in Heaven: A Reconsideration of *Paradise Lost*, III. 1–417", *Proceedings of the Modern Language Association of America*, 72 (1957), 601–11.

———. "*Paradise Lost* as Mimesis", in *Approaches to Paradise Lost*, ed. C. A. Patrides (London, 1968), pp. 15–29.

Sherry, Beverley. "Milton's Raphael and the Legend of Tobias", *Journal of English and Germanic Philology*, 78 (1979), 233–47.

Swaim, Kathleen M. "Hercules, Antaeus, and Prometheus: A Study of the Climactic Epic Similes in *Paradise Regained*", *Studies in English Literature*, 18 (1978), 137–53.

Index